# Advance Praise for *The Portable Film School*

"Just when you think there aren't any more books to write about film-making, here comes D. B. Gilles's *The Portable Film School,* a wonderful on-paper process that shows you how to write screenplays and make both short and long films. Ideal for anyone who doesn't go to film school."

    —Lew Hunter, screenwriter, author of *Lew Hunter's Screenwriting 434,* and UCLA screenwriting professor and chair emeritus

"D. B. Gilles is a writer and teacher who knows what he's talking about. Amazingly, he's willing to tell everybody else, and in the most straightforward, no-BS, useful way imaginable. *The Portable Film School* will save you years of head-scratching and will completely demystify the process of making a movie. Everything you need to know is here; you'll only have to supply the guts and a good story."

    —Christopher Vogler, former FOX development executive and author of *The Writer's Journey: Mythic Structure for Writers*

"Savvy, incisive, and funny, D. B. Gilles's latest walks you through every piece of advice you're likely to hear at film school. An excellent starter set for the fledgling filmmaker."

    —David McKenna, professor at Columbia University, Film Division

"*The Portable Film School* should be mandatory reading not just for those unable to go to film school, but for anyone thinking about it or even currently attending it. A detailed and knowledgeable how-to."

    —David Benullo, former student and cowriter of the screenplay for *Around the World in 80 Days*

# The Portable
# Film School

## ALSO BY D. B. GILLES

### Nonfiction

*The Screenwriter Within:*
*How to Turn the Movie in Your Head into a Salable Screenplay*

### Humor

*W. The First 100 Days: A White House Journal*
(with Sheldon Woodbury)

### Plays

*Cash Flow*
*Men's Singles*
*The Legendary Stardust Boys*
*The Girl Who Loved the Beatles*

### Screenplays

*Thinly Disguised*
*I Remember You*
*The Movie Lovers*
*Living Proof*

# The Portable Film School

Everything You'd Learn in Film School
(Without Ever Going to Class)

## D. B. Gilles

St. Martin's Griffin

New York

www.stmartins.com

Library of Congress Cataloging-in-Publication Data

Gilles, D. B.
    The portable film school : everything you'd learn in film school (without ever going to class) / D. B. Gilles.–1st St. Martin's Griffin ed.
        p. cm.
    ISBN 0-312-34738-3
    EAN 978-0-312-34738-3
    1. Motion pictures–Production and direction.  2. Motion picture authorship.
I. Title.
PN1995.9.P7G444 2005
791.4302'3–dc22

                                                                    2005010404

20   19

*For my mother,*
*Josephine Gilles*

*Very special thanks to
friend and filmmaker
Andrew Stoeckley*

# Contents

# Acknowledgments

To my muse, Jane Campbell; my consigliere, Don DeMaio; and my script consultant, Sheldon Woodbury. To Nick Stevens for his wise counsel; my agent, Jane Dystel; my editor, Sheila Curry Oakes; and my copy editor, Barbara Wild.

Teaching in the Undergraduate Film and Television Department at New York University's Tisch School of the Arts has given me the privilege of working with enormously talented people. I want to thank all my colleagues, specifically David Irving, Lamar Sanders, Paul Thompson, Nick Tanis, James Gardner, Rick Litvin, Ezra Sacks, Peter Rea, Mo Ogrodnick, Dean Sheril Antonio, and Wendy Kaplan, for always answering my questions.

A big thanks also to my sister Kathy for always being there for me.

And to Lou Stalsworth and Sharon Schapow: getting it right this time.

Drama is life with the dull bits cut out.

−ALFRED HITCHCOCK

# Part I

# Curriculum

# When Film School Isn't an Option

When you go to a university film school you start by learning how to tell stories. You move up to writing short screenplays and learning how to direct your scripts. The next step is writing a full-length screenplay.

What you will find within the covers of this book is a film school in a nutshell. You'll learn the fundamental skills and techniques of screenwriting and moviemaking. You will also learn how to make a short film without going broke in the process.

Like film students in formal programs you'll begin by learning how to tell a story.

Then you'll write a few short screenplays of between five and ten pages.

After that you'll go through the process of producing and directing one of those scripts.

Last, you'll move on to writing a full-length screenplay.

Your goal is to create a compelling film under ten minutes long to show off your abilities as a director and a full-length screenplay to demonstrate your skills as a writer.

Whatever your age, starting now, think of yourself as a student. You're about to experience the next best thing to being in film school.

The best students are open to suggestion. You don't know what you don't know. Receive. Keep an open mind.

You'll work hard, but remember the old saying: "The bitterness of studying is preferable to the bitterness of ignorance."

Once you learn how to do something well, you will no longer be a beginner. As you develop skills, you'll move forward and keep getting better. Storytelling, filmmaking, and screenwriting are the skills that you will learn in *The Portable Film School.*

Once you understand them your goal is to master them. Much like an apprentice in the Middle Ages, you'll learn by doing until *you* become a master.

Others have done it.

You can, too!

## Colloquium

# Why All Screenwriters Are Directors

The study of dramatic structure should
start rigidly and advance to flexibility.
–KENNETH THORPE ROWE

Half of the screenwriters I've met have little or no interest in directing their screenplays. They simply want to write their script and hope that they get a deal and somebody else will direct it.

They think this way because they assume that all their creative energy should be channeled into their writing and that directing is some kind of mystical higher calling.

What these screenwriters don't realize is that when they sit down to write their screenplay they're already "directing" it in their heads. They're acting it, too, probably saying the dialogue they write to themselves as it pours out.

By virtue of the fact that a screenwriter says–

**INT. KITCHEN–DAY**

–he has made a decision as to where the scene will take place. If the kitchen is that of a woman who is a gourmet cook, he might describe the kitchen like this:

**INT. KITCHEN—DAY**
State-of-the-art   oven   and   refrigerator.
Copper  pots  and  pans  hang  from  a  ceiling
rack. Numerous chef tools and gadgets. Elab-
orate  spice  rack  filled  with  three  dozen
spices. Plenty of counter space. A window
looks out onto a sprawling backyard where we
see a garden of fresh herbs and vegetables.
Two dozen cookbooks line one wall shelf.

Or...

Let's say you decide that the person doesn't know how to cook,
seldom uses her kitchen, and lives in a studio apartment. The description could easily read like this:

**INT. KITCHEN—DAY**
Tiny. Windowless. Neat. A small teakettle on
the stove.

I could describe five or ten variations on a kitchen to create a
sense of whose kitchen it is, to convey something (or several things)
about the user of this kitchen, and each would be different and
unique. How many kitchens have you been in? Have you ever seen
two kitchens that looked (or smelled) alike? I haven't.

So, depending upon how much the person I'm writing about uses
her kitchen, depending upon how important her kitchen is to her, depending upon what I want this woman's kitchen to convey about her—
to make a visual statement about her (that she's a gourmet cook, that
she's sloppy, that she likes gadgets, that she likes to wear aprons
with funny sayings on them) I will describe the kitchen accordingly.

Not only am I *writing* the scene; I'm also directing it. First in my
head, then on the page.

Most screenwriting courses and books discourage the screenwriter from including camera angles and shots, largely because it's assumed that the script will be directed by somebody else, so the screenwriter should allow the *real* director to determine where to place the camera to film each scene.

I agree with this thinking to a certain extent, but only from the point of view that filling a script with dozens upon dozens of camera angles and needlessly long stage directions is a surefire way to not get your script read.

However, to tell *this* particular story about this woman who likes to cook, it's important to describe the kitchen in a specific way.

Here's why: She's going to murder her husband. More about that in a bit.

The basic questions a director must deal with are where to put the camera and what to tell the actors.

As a screenwriter, you don't have to talk to actors or figure out whether to place the camera shooting upward, downward, or in a straight-on master shot. That's literally the job of the director when the film is being shot. And if you turn out to be the one directing your screenplay, you will have to deal with that eventually.

But as you sit at your computer or, if you write in longhand, you're staring at your notebook page, as the screenwriter you have to decide on three basic things:

1. Where is it set?
2. Who will be in the scene?
3. What is the dramatic purpose of the scene?

Back to this woman who likes to cook and is going to murder her husband.

Let's say she's twenty-eight, unhappily married to a successful, womanizing stockbroker, and lives in a great house in an upscale suburb. Her only pleasure and form of creative expression is cooking. She spends lots of time in her kitchen, so it's very important that you describe her kitchen as one that looks like the kitchen of a person who loves to cook.

**INT. SUBURBAN KITCHEN–DAY**
Spacious, with state-of-the-art equipment and gadgets.

Just saying this isn't enough.

That description *would* be enough if the woman hated to cook, if her kitchen wasn't crucial to the story, or if only one scene took place in the kitchen and that was simply to have someone go into it to get a glass of water.

But because the story we're writing is about *this* twenty-eight-year-old gourmet cook who has decided to *murder* her philandering husband with one of her expensive, professional-caliber knives . . . the kitchen is more than the setting for a scene. It's become one of the characters.

Who will be in the scene depends on the scene. You can introduce your main character by having her alone in her kitchen, skimming through a cookbook and watching a cooking show on the TV mounted over the spacious counter. Or you can show her chopping vegetables so we see how adept she is. Or you can have her talking to a visiting friend.

You can write whatever you choose to have her doing in order to establish her world, her proficiency as a cook, and perhaps her unhappiness. In doing so you've met the requirements of a scene:

- Where is it set? (The kitchen)
- Who's in it? (The main character and her best friend)
- What is the scene's dramatic purpose? (To show the main character's interest and proficiency at cooking *and that she has a big chef knife*)

There might be ten or twenty scenes in this kitchen, but each will have a different dramatic purpose.

As the screenwriter, you've made some choices about structure and dialogue. But the voice of the Director in Your Head will have other ideas.

That Directorial Voice isn't concerned with what the characters say but rather what they do. And the Directorial Voice will be more concerned with showing objects that will further the plot or make a statement about the character.

For example, the screenwriter in you might write a stage direction like:

```
She reaches into a drawer, removes an expen-
sive chef knife and begins chopping a bell
pepper with great expertise.
```

The Directorial Voice would do it differently:

```
She reaches into a drawer, removes a 9" chef
knife from Wusthof.

CUT TO:
The knife's blade. She presses her index fin-
ger against it.

CUT TO:
A whetstone on the counter. She proceeds to
sharpen the knife purposefully.

CUT TO:
Her face. As she sharpens the knife she has
a menacing look.
```

**CUT TO:**
A luscious red bell pepper. Her hand comes
into frame. Grabs the pepper.

**CUT TO:**
A cutting board. The red bell pepper is po-
sitioned on the cutting board.

**CUT TO:**
The knife chopping quickly, expertly.

The difference between a screenwriter and a director is that the director will find ways to dramatize what the writer has put on the page.
He will accomplish this by deciding which series of shots will best
achieve this.

The advantage of directing your own screenplay is that you can
decide upon *every* shot in the script. When you're writing a screenplay for someone else to direct, you have to be more selective about
your stage directions. Concentrate on the dialogue (if there is any)
and the emotional intent of what's happening in the scene.

Write every scene the way you see it in your head. You're not only
writing; you're directing.

# Part II

# Storytelling

**Story:** A usually fictional prose or
verse narrative intended to interest or amuse
the hearer or reader; a tale.
*–THE AMERICAN HERITAGE DICTIONARY*

**Story-teller:** One who tells
stories; a narrator of anecdotes, incidents, or
fictitious tales; as, an amusing story-teller.
*–WEBSTER'S REVISED UNABRIDGED DICTIONARY*

## Lecture 1

# First Get the Story,
# Then Worry About How to Tell It

Don't wait for experience to come to you;
go out after experience. Experience is your material.
—W. SOMERSET MAUGHAM

Lawyers will tell you that the first commandment of the legal profession is "First get the case."

I think it's fair to say that the first commandment of screenwriting and filmmaking should be "First get the story."

What exactly is this thing called a story?

Many new screenwriters (of all ages) have no problem finding situations, but when it comes to actual stories they often come up lacking.

What's the difference between a situation and a story?

SITUATION: A girl and a guy are sitting on a bench.

STORY: A girl and a guy are sitting on a bench and the girl is trying to find the courage to break up with him because she has fallen in love with another guy.

The story has the potential for drama. The situation is nothing except a scene in which nothing is happening.

If you want to crank up the potential for drama, toss in the following sentence:

... because she has fallen in love with his best friend.

Or ...

... because she has fallen in love with his sister.

Or ...

... because she's been lying to him all along and she's really a man.

These scenarios are ripe for development into stories. You can see the potential for drama.

Every screenplay must have this potential for drama, from the dumbest comedy to the most heartbreaking tragedy. Look at the 2003 independent film *The Station Agent.* The main character is an antisocial dwarf. Two people try to befriend him, but he is standoffish until gradually contact is made. The story of this very small but engaging film is difficult to describe.

The dwarf's boss dies and leaves him an abandoned train station in his will. The dwarf, who is a nut about trains, decides to leave the city where he lives and take up residence in the train station, which is pretty much a dump. (Sounds like a real winner so far, eh?) Anyway, a woman almost runs the dwarf down in her car. As she attempts to apologize to him, she reaches out to him. So does a guy who operates a food cart across from the train station. Just as the dwarf is virtually silent through much of the film, the food cart guy never shuts up.

The potential for drama among these three people is what holds our interest.

As the story unfolds, they come together, they argue, they part, the dwarf loses his cool in a bar, we find out information about the woman and the food cart guy, and ultimately—although not a lot has happened—there is a satisfying ending.

What held our attention was not the situation of a dwarf who inherits an abandoned train station in the middle of nowhere but its potential for drama.

## Okay, You've Found the Story—But Is It Big Enough?

Let's say you go camping one weekend. While there you trip on a rock and sprain your ankle. And you lose your can opener. Spraining your ankle probably hurt and not having a can opener most likely made opening the canned goods you brought with you impossible. When you come back you might be able to entertain your friends with how your camping trip was tainted because of your ankle sprain and lost can opener. But as you tell the story you probably won't have your audience listening with bated breath.

However, if your story was that you went camping one weekend and were attacked by a bear and your two companions were kidnapped by Bigfoot you'd have a rapt audience.

That's why people write short scripts and make short films. Stories don't necessarily have to be huge. In fact, a short film about a guy who goes camping and loses his can opener might be interesting to watch as he finds ways to open the cans.

The story is simply: Will the guy find a way to open the cans so he can eat and not starve?

It's interesting, but it's not big enough to sustain dramatic tension for 110 pages.

Screenwriters about to embark on their first script tend to have

I always encourage my students to shoot for 110 pages. For many years the conventional length has been 120 pages, and this is still true, for the most part. However, I've found that by telling a screenwriter who may have problems with overwriting to complete his script sooner, it helps him edit himself. Likewise, for screenwriters who tend to underwrite, the 110-page finish line gives them a goal to aim for.

problems finding stories to tell. More often than not they fall into the trap of writing what they know. Despite the numerous books on writing novels, plays, short stories, and screenplays that tell you to "write what you know," this advice can be misleading.

Writing what you know is often misinterpreted to mean "write what you have experienced."

Well, that's cool to do, as long as you aren't writing about something *exactly* the way it happened.

I recall one particular student who was incapable of writing anything that she hadn't experienced. She was divorced, so she wrote about her divorce. She had an abusive father, so she wrote about her abusive father. She had an affair with her boss, so she wrote about having an affair with her boss.

When she would bring pages into class and certain scenes or bits of dialogue were questioned by others or me, she would say, "But that's exactly how it happened." This would lead to a discussion on just how much of what "really happened" should make it into the script.

I told her that if she wrote it too close to the way it happened, she wouldn't be writing a screenplay; she'd be writing a documentary.

The best advice I ever heard on using your life to fuel fiction came from a wonderful book on playwriting called *Write That Play,* by Kenneth Thorpe Rowe, published in 1939 and now, unfortunately, out of print. He said: "Life is not transferred to fiction but transformed."

So don't hesitate to write about what you've experienced, but make sure you take the emotional essence and not the actual experience or you'll be making a documentary, not an engaging film.

## Lecture 2

# Don't Be Intimidated by Rules— Embrace Them

> You don't have a choice about writing
> the story. There's a filter at work
> which says this is or is not a story. . . .
> I think a story ideally comes to the writer.
> —RAYMOND CARVER

Rules are the best friends of anyone who wants to write and make movies.

Although it may not seem like it when you're starting out, learning the rules and understanding how to apply them already makes you better and puts you ahead of the person who's busy rebelling against the "old-fashioned" way of doing things.

Don't think of rules as regimentation. Start to look at rules as the things you must learn in order to develop technique.

You get technique from practicing the rules.

It's like cooking.

Many filmmakers are self-taught, just as many great cooks are.

Let's pretend you don't want to be a screenwriter or filmmaker but that you're interested in becoming a chef.

At first, you'll be following recipes exactly. Measuring ingredients and oven temperatures and whatnot, just like the recipes say you should. But once you become more familiar and comfortable with a recipe you'll seldom, if ever, look at it again. You've become confident enough to improvise, to know your own taste buds and respect your own judgment.

If you've ever watched cooking shows on PBS or the Food Network, you'll see that chefs all chop onions the way they learned to do it at cooking school. There's a bunch of different ways to chop an onion, but there's only one right way to do it and get a nice, even texture without cutting yourself.

## Exercise

Cut an onion in half. Trim off the ends. Put the flat side down. Make two or three sideways incisions, spin it around, and cut through, always making sure that your fingertips are folded toward your palm and protected.

Watch any chefs on the Food Network or PBS chop onions and you'll see that they all do it the same way.

It's the same with screenwriters and filmmakers who have grasped the rules and apply them to their work. They all will make different types of movies, but the fundamentals remain.

## Twelve Storytelling Musts

- There must be a story.
- Every story must have an *Instigating Event*. Think of this as the thing that happens that makes the rest of the movie happen. Someone is murdered. A woman finds out her husband is having an affair. A college-bound basketball star breaks his leg and loses his scholarship. A boy meets a girl. Someone is kidnapped. The Instigating Event leads to:

- *The Major Dramatic Question.* Will they find the killer? What will the woman do? What will the basketball star's future be without the scholarship? Will the boy and girl overcome all obstacles and get together? Will they get the ransom to the kidnapper in time? Ideally, the Major Dramatic Question must come as soon as possible. Another way of thinking about this is: The Major Dramatic Question asks what the main character *wants.*

- He must have a "want." *The Want* is what motivates all of the character's actions throughout the script, until he gets what he wants. If he gets what he wants at the end of the script, the movie ends. However, sometimes he will get what he wants earlier, perhaps at the end of Act Two. Then he must deal with the consequences of getting his "want," which may lead to his "wanting" something else.

- Things can never be too easy for your main character. There must be plenty of complications, adversaries, and obstacles.

- There must be an ally (or allies) to help the main character overcome obstacles.

- The hero must fail before he succeeds.

- There must be a dramatic moment or event in the middle of Act Two that turns up the heat of the story a few more degrees.

- There must be some crucial piece of new information two-thirds of the way into the story, usually at the end of Act Two. This is known as the Turning Point or, to get fancy, *peripety* (from the Greek: a sudden and unexpected change of fortune or reverse of circumstances [especially in a literary work]; a peripeteia swiftly turns a routine sequence of events into a story worth telling [WordNet 2.0, August 2003]).

- No matter what the genre, the last third of the script—Act Three—must be the most exciting and interesting. Think of

Acts One and Two as the ride up a roller coaster and Act Three as the ride down.

- There must be change or arc in the main character's personality that brings him to a different, presumably better, place than he was at the start of the story, i.e., ignorant to knowledgeable, prejudiced to tolerant, or politically incorrect to politically correct. In real life people may not change, but in art they must.

- The ending doesn't necessarily have to be happy or sad but must be satisfying.

**Lecture 3**

# Some of Your Best Ideas
# Will Come from Other People

You do not need to leave your room.
Remain sitting at your table and listen.
Do not even listen, simply wait, be quite
still and solitary. The world will freely
offer itself to you to be unmasked, it
has no choice, it will roll in ecstasy at your feet.

—FRANZ KAFKA

Ideas often come out of nowhere. They just show up when you are going about your daily life. And I don't mean only ideas for screenplays. You might get an idea for a character or for a way to give a weak character some shadings and contours while you're stuck in a traffic jam.

Shadings and contours are the things that give depth to a character. The way you come to see these nuances can be: You overhear a conversation. Someone tells you an anecdote. You observe a stranger's odd or amusing habits.

These are gifts. It's not as if you're stealing somebody's material. You just happen to be in the right place at the right time.

There's a woman in my building who always talks about movies. She says hello and starts talking about the latest movie she has seen. There's never any other dialogue exchanged. She asks if I saw such-

and-such and I say yes or no. If I say yes we have a brief exchange. If I say no she encourages me to see it. She does this with other people, too.

I think it's kind of quirky and amusing. I may use this someday. In fact, I just did by telling you.

See? A perfect example of something I observed that I could use.

Then there's the middle-aged lawyer I know who's very friendly and soft-spoken. Unfortunately, he stinks. I mean, the guy is ripe! He smells worse than ground meat left out in the sun for three days in a pair of Shaquille O'Neal's unwashed sweat socks.

There are the cross-eyed deli guys. I once lived in a neighborhood with a deli in which all the people who worked were cross-eyed. I don't mean just lazy eyes or droopy eyelids; I mean full-blown cross-eyed and walleyed individuals. It was funny. Not laugh out loud funny but, well, amusing in an insensitive kind of way that makes you feel guilty for laughing. By the fifth time I went in I no longer noticed. It's another one of those oddball things I've filed away.

I can't leave out the porter in my apartment building who retired a couple of years ago. Guy was probably in his midfifties. Decent sort, always friendly. His job was to clean up and to put out the garbage. One day the building management announces that the porter's going to retire after thirty years. A lot of tenants gave him gifts of cash for his long service. A few weeks later the information comes out that the

---

### Speaking of Filing Away Ideas . . .

Some writers carry notebooks to write down lines, stories, situations, titles, and so on, and others don't. I've always had a notebook, but I'm constantly misplacing it. I have a file on my computer called "IDEAS," in which I stick everything that pops into my head for possible use down the road. The good thing about a computer file is that you always know where it is.

guy is a millionaire three times over. Turns out he spent all these years collecting the bottles from the building and cashing them in for small change. He lived simply. Never went on vacations or out to dinner. Saved every cent. By the time he retired he was wealthier than, dare I say, most of the people in the building.

Finally there's the female shoemaker in my neighborhood. I broke a lace on my Timberlands and couldn't find the right-sized lace anywhere, so I stopped into the shoemaker down the street. I go in and see this woman, maybe late twenties. Pretty. Could be Italian or Greek. Thick, shoulder-length black hair. I'm thinking she's the owner's daughter or wife or the bookkeeper.

Then I looked at her fingers. They were stained with shoe polish. I realize that *she's* the shoemaker.

I'm immediately thinking that there's a movie here. Uptight, affluent Yuppie from Connecticut and all the right schools falls in love with a female shoemaker.

Maybe a variation on *Moonstruck.* Definitely a romantic comedy. I know: *Moonstruck* meets *My Big Fat Greek Wedding.* She's not wearing a wedding ring, so presumably she's single. What does she do about her stained fingers when she has a date? My mind starts working. Why doesn't she wear gloves when she works? Is she self-conscious about the way her hands look? How does she feel being a shoemaker? How did she get into the profession? I wonder if winter is her favorite time of year because she can wear gloves more often. Another time I saw her opening the shop. She rides a bike to work. Is she ever attracted to the men who bring her their shoes to have heel and sole replacements? Does she have an uncanny ability to judge people by the shoes they wear?

There are so many possibilities that come from this woman.

I can give at least twenty more examples of the quirky habits and behavior of people in my building and neighborhood. If you're observant enough you can find things in your world, too.

I challenge you to top the female shoemaker.

**Lecture 4**

# Four Short Writing Exercises That You Might Think Are Stupid and a Waste of Time but Aren't (Trust Me)

I carry my ideas about me for a long time,
often a very long time, before
I commit them to writing.
–LUDWIG VAN BEETHOVEN

Finding the story you want to tell is the first stage of the writing process and, for some, the most difficult.

You should be looking for stories that can be filmed. Some stories are good for anecdotes or amusing yarns you tell to a friend in a coffee shop or during a phone call.

"Boy, did I have fun last night researching the eating habits of Henry VIII's wives. Who knew that venison was Anne Boleyn's favorite meat and that kidney pie was her late-night comfort food of choice?"

Probably not that cinematic.

Whether it's an eight-minute short or full-length, screenplays need to be stories that can be told through film.

If you have an idea about an eighteen-year-old boy in Kansas who's about to break up with his girlfriend the night before he leaves for college in Philadelphia and you've set it on her front porch at midnight, well, that would probably work better as a ten-minute play.

Sure, you can point a camera in front of them as they sit on the porch and film them talking. Maybe you can have a few shots of her running away hysterically and him chasing her into the backyard. Or her following him as he heads toward his car.

Ultimately it's a two-character play about a guy breaking up with a girl.

That's the difference between a play and a screenplay. Plays are words. Lots of words that actors say. Screenplays are fewer words and lots of images. Writers who like to have their characters talk and through the dialogue tell a story should be playwrights. Writers who like their characters to say fewer words in dozens of short spurts in numerous locations to tell a story should be screenwriters. That's why most playwrights tend to shy away from screenplays and screenwriters tend to shy away from plays. They are different genres. However, that's not to say that one can't do both.

One thing a screenplay and certainly a film do more than a play is utilize the concept of place.

To wit:

## Exercise #1: Write an Eight-Page Screenplay Where *Place* Is a Central Character

I'll provide the place and the situation. You write the script.

### A Funeral Home

What if there are two bodies laid out in different viewing rooms at a funeral home? A hot twenty-year-old girl's uncle has died, and so did the aunt of a twenty-year-old guy. Let's say that neither kid was especially fond of his or her deceased aunt or uncle. But their parents make them go to the funeral home to pay their respects.

Notwithstanding the success of HBO's *Six Feet Under,* if there's one place in the world that isn't conducive to romance, it's a funeral home. Nobody in his right mind would expect to meet someone under these circumstances.

In this short writing exercise you're going to chronicle how these two meet. Take advantage of the place in every scene. Since you'll only be writing this and not filming it, write it as if cost is not an issue.

You can create the two characters any way you want. All I'm providing is their ages.

If you were in a class with twelve other people, each of you would write this short exercise differently. You would each make choices. Since this exercise focuses on place, someone might begin with a fade in shot establishing the funeral home or a close-up of the sign in the front yard. Someone else might fade in on a hearse parked in the back. Or five hearses. Someone else might fade in on the face of a body in a coffin.

The point is, there are many ways to go and no right way.

Take your shot!

Then, for additional practice, choose your own place and write a short screenplay around it.

By having an understanding of place, you'll be able to write dialogue more specifically.

For example, a dialogue between two women in the backyard gardening and talking about their marriages will have a different spin if they are working out together at their health club or volunteering at a soup kitchen.

## Exercise #2:
## Write a Five-Page Internal Monologue Screenplay

An internal monologue means your character is talking to herself. Every line of dialogue we hear is what she is thinking. We must never hear her speak a word.

I'll provide the situation again:

## The Person Is Running Late to an Important Appointment

Chronicle her movements from the moment she wakes up (late, of course) until she arrives at her destination.

For example, the fade in shot might be a close-up of the person's face as her cat is licking her cheek. She wakes up, fusses over the cat for a second, then calmly looks at the alarm clock and realizes to her horror that it hasn't gone off.

Note: The following dialogue is pretty bad.
I wrote it strictly as an example.

> GIRL
> (thinking)

Damn!

She jumps out of bed.

> GIRL
> (thinking)
> Why did I have that fourth margarita?

She rushes to the bathroom, pulling her nightgown off. She stubs her toe on her dresser, screams in pain, catches a glimpse of herself in the mirror.

> GIRL
> (thinking)
> I look like shit.

**INT. BATHROOM—DAY**
She jolts into the bathroom. Turns on the shower. Starts to get in, but stops.

>                    GIRL
>                 (thinking)
>    No way. I'll just wash my face.

She quickly turns on the cold water in the sink.

**INT. BEDROOM-DAY**
She's getting dressed. Slips into one shoe. Can't find the other. Flips open the closet door. Falls to her knees. Starts sorting through all her shoes.

>                    GIRL
>                 (thinking)
>    Where is it? Where is it?

Finds a <u>different</u> shoe. Smiles.

>                    GIRL
>                 (thinking)
>    I wondered where you've been.

You get the idea. Now you do one.


## Exercise #3: Create a Character History

Creating a character is the easiest, hardest thing in the world. All you have to do is establish a pattern of habits and behavior.

That's all! Easy, right?

Not exactly!

How do you define a pattern of habits or behavior?

Someone is always late for work, for appointments, for dinner with friends—for *everything*. He also is inordinately charming. So charming, in fact, that everyone always forgives him for being late. In fact, he's forgiven for every bad, rude, or inconsiderate thing he does.

Consequently, he takes things for granted. He never once considers the consequences of his actions.

He's also cheap. He never picks up a tab, is always short of cash, and is constantly bumming money off of his friends and family. To top it off he's a spendthrift. He likes clothes. What money he does have he blows on the latest styles at the most expensive men's stores.

Let's take it to the next level. Someone's pattern of behavior is to lie and cheat. He started lying and cheating in first grade, and because he's very convincing he's able to get away with lots of stuff. This works for him throughout middle school and into high school, but along the way he also added stealing to his repertoire.

So he lies, cheats, and steals. Presumably he'll lie to his parents about where he's going. He'll lie to his girlfriend. He'll cheat on his girlfriend. He'll steal money from his aunt's purse when she's visiting for Thanksgiving dinner. He'll steal a copy of an important test so he can cheat on it. When he gets a part-time job he'll steal from his employer: money or office supplies or whatever he can get his hands on.

He goes to college. Pays other people to do his papers or steals his roommate's notes. He's still lying to and cheating on his girlfriends.

He gets older. Marries. Cheats on his wife. Cheats on his taxes. He teaches his child how to get away with things.

This is a clear pattern of behavior—bad behavior.

It's just as easy to create a life scenario of someone who has behaved honorably and with integrity. Look at your own habits and behavior. You know your good points and bad.

Take a sheet of paper and make a list of your bad behavior and habits (too much smoking, drinking, eating junk food, and so on), as well as your strengths and the things you'd like to change about yourself.

You will discover who you are.

Ironically, it's the character with bad or questionable behavior that's somehow more engaging to watch. The religious, friendly, modest librarian who volunteers to work with sick children and visits the local nursing home might be an honorable human being, but her twin sister the stripper in Las Vegas who parties with rock stars, hangs out with Paris Hilton, and is the mistress of a multimillionaire tycoon who owns a casino is probably more interesting.

Maybe not. Although on the surface the librarian seems to be leading a more wholesome life, what if she's filled with rage and anger internally? What if she was molested as a child? Or raped when she was in college? What if she's hiding from the real world behind her religion and good works? What if? What if? What if?

And what if underneath all the glitz, her stripper sister is really the "better," more well-adjusted person?

## Assignment

After you've found out more about yourself, create a character history of someone you'd like to be the lead in a short screenplay you'll write. The history can be as long or short as your imagination dictates. Stop writing when you've come up with enough information about the person to get a sense of who he or she is. Then give the character a name. Once you start referring to a character, especially your lead, by name it helps make him or her come alive.

## Exercise #4: Find Five Dramatic Situations That Would Make Good Short Screenplays

Generating ideas isn't as difficult as you might think, provided you understand that the nature of drama is for someone to want something that is unattainable without great effort or that some people are victimized by life and must deal with an unexpected blow.

Here's five examples. You come up with five more.

- A guy lends his new girlfriend his favorite novel, which she doesn't get around to reading. A few months pass. They break up. He forgets she has his favorite book until one day he wants it back.

  THE STORY: How will he go about getting back his favorite book?

- A six-foot-seven seventeen-year-old boy with aspirations of winning a basketball scholarship and playing in the NBA injures his knee beyond repair and must accept the fact that he'll never play college or professional basketball.

  THE STORY: He must come to terms with the reality that his dream can never be and must find a new goal. Or: He must decide that his doctors are wrong and become determined to play again. Will he succeed?

- A deeply religious single middle-aged Catholic woman falls in love with the new priest assigned to her parish, which forces her to question her faith. When he makes it clear that he has feelings for her as well, she is torn between pursuing her heart and following her religious convictions.

  THE STORY: Will she have a romantic relationship with the priest or not?

- A guy begins dating a girl from a warm, loving family. She gets along great with her parents and is especially close to her father. One day the guy spots his girlfriend's father with another woman.

  THE STORY: Does the guy tell his girlfriend or pretend he knows nothing?

- A girl finds a wallet on the street that contains seven hundred dollars. She has big money problems. The money will come in handy. The wallet belongs to an elderly woman. Along with the seven hundred dollars is a stub from a Social Security check. The girl realizes that this is probably the only income the elderly lady has.

THE STORY: Does the girl keep the money to solve her own financial problems or does she return the cash to the elderly woman? Or: Does the girl use the cash for her own needs and promise to pay the woman back somehow?

Now *you* come up with five dramatic situations. Will you ever write any of them? Probably not. There's no right or wrong way of doing this exercise. Its purpose is to get you in the habit of always being on the lookout for ideas and figuring out how to dramatize them.

This should become a habit, especially when you move on to full-length screenplays. An idea pops into your head—maybe only a sentence, a vague notion, or a situation. By writing it down and figuring out what the story is you've taken the first step toward turning it into a script.

## Lecture 5

# Writing the Short Screenplay: Don't Run a Marathon Before You Do Wind Sprints

We create our path by walking.
—BUDDHIST SAYING

Maybe you've heard this before: "Don't run before you can walk."

This wisdom applies to screenwriting big-time. In film school you start by writing several short screenplays to get a feel for the genre. Then you progress to shooting one. That's what we're going to do here, too.

Be patient. I know you want to get cracking on a full-length screenplay, and you will, soon. However, that experience will be substantially less difficult if you take some time to learn a few fundamentals and tricks of the screenwriting trade.

The first fundamental is to have a story. Preferably one that is compelling. More on that in a minute.

Another expression you've heard before is: "Practice makes perfect."

Translated to screenwriting, that means the more you write, the better you'll get.

Your biggest problem will be finding material to write about. I've come in contact with thousands of screenwriters over the years, and the one thing they have in common is the ability to find ideas. Not necessarily *good* ideas but any ideas.

A minority of the screenwriters I've known are never at a loss for material. They have index cards or files filled with ideas for stories. The rest are, let's say, in between ideas. If they're lucky, they get one or two a year. They may have plenty of situations but no concrete stories.

All writers experience writer's block at some point, and they all eventually get through it.

Not being able to come up with ideas is more of a creativity block.

This type of block is when you just can't come up with even an inkling of a snippet of a notion of an idea to turn into a screenplay, be it full-length or less than ten pages.

Because I'm advocating that you take your first steps as a screenwriter by writing a few short screenplays, it's my belief that it'll be "easier" (and I use the term loosely) to find ideas for the short form than for full-length.

If this was a book about teaching yourself to play tennis, I'd suggest that you play for an hour every day.

I'm suggesting that you write every day. It doesn't have to be for a long period of time. If you can commit to an hour—even half an hour—a day, it's a good start.

Basically, you need to develop a pattern of discipline, not only for writing but also for discovering ideas.

Famed Massachusetts congressman Tip O'Neill once said, "All politics is local." I believe that many of the stories we tell are local, too, in that we write about things that have moved us or are important to us.

When you're new to the screenwriting game and it comes to writing a short screenplay, say anywhere from five to fifteen pages, your best bet for finding an idea is to go local.

Look inside your head. Better yet, your heart.

When in doubt, always go within. Stories lurk there. Stories may arise from experiences you've buried. Fears. Embarrassing things you or your friends have done.

No matter how young you are, you have a history of experiences, observations, and hearsay (anecdotes and stories you've heard) to draw from.

However, from my classroom experience, I know that it can take weeks for someone to come up with a compelling idea. That's why in many of my classes I provide the premises for short writing exercises. It helps students to focus immediately on how to tell the story.

In the words of Dr. Laurence J. Peter, author of *The Peter Principle,* "If you don't know where you're going, you'll probably end up somewhere else."

However, with a solid premise as a starting point and a basic outline you will know *exactly* where you're going.

You've probably noticed that this is the second exercise I've suggested revolving around death. This is intentional, because there's nothing in life more serious, emotional, and *filled with drama* than death. A short film about a boy and girl who meet at Burger King or in the sweater section of Banana Republic is somehow not as compelling or challenging to write.

Anyway, before you start writing, here are a few questions you'll need to think about:

Has anyone you loved died? Parent, sibling, relative, best friend,

---

### Basic Premise

Your main character must tell someone about the death of a loved one. Your main character is reluctant to do this because it's such a difficult thing to do. But there is no one else to do the job. Your main character is afraid of how the person he tells will react to the news, afraid because the person might fall apart or get overly emotional. Your main character doesn't handle others' emotions well.

pet. Remember how you felt? Or you might be someone who hasn't yet lost someone you loved. If that's the case, think about other people you've known who've lost someone. If that doesn't work, imagine what it would be like to lose someone you love.

If you did lose someone, try to recall how you felt when you heard the news.

Were you sad? Shocked? Overcome with grief? Numb? You must have felt something. Or maybe you felt ambivalent or happy, because you hated the person. Even disinterest is a feeling.

I was ten years old when my grandmother died. Not only do I still remember waking up that morning and having my mother tell me; I can also visualize it in my head, even to the point of remembering what my mother was wearing and the intonation of her voice.

Maybe you have an equally strong memory of a personal loss. Use it. But remember, you are not writing a memoir. Using your experience and the emotions it generates helps you to write a more compelling, realistic story.

## Suggested Structure (Feel Free to Find Your Own)

- Your main character finds out someone has died. (Instigating Event)
- He's told that he must tell someone else about the death. He resists, protesting that he shouldn't have to do it, but he must. (He becomes your Reluctant Hero.)
- He faces up to the fact that he must do it and sets out to make it so. (Major Dramatic Question: Will he do it and if so, what will the consequences be?)

Now give it a go.

## Assignment

As soon as you finish the story, start thinking of your own original idea for a short screenplay—ten pages long—ideally something you will direct and make yourself. I recommend using a small cast (no more than four people), as few sets as possible, and, for economic reasons, mostly outdoor locations.

Shooting indoors is more involved because you need lights. You can easily shoot outdoors without lights and it will look nice, but indoors the lighting is completely up to you. Of course, shooting outdoors presents you with the problems of weather, traffic, noises that might interfere with sound recording, pedestrians who are too curious about what you're doing, and overall greater danger to cast, crew, and equipment, since outdoor sequences can involve shots that you wouldn't usually do indoors like running, and so forth. Not to mention, in the summer spending a day outdoors can be quite exhausting. (Bring lots of water.)

Come up with a plot that has a clear Instigating Event and Major Dramatic Question that gets answered by the last page.

Once you write this script, move on to the next lecture.

**Lecture 6**

# How to Rewrite Your Short Screenplay (Despite the Fact That You Think It's Perfect)

First drafts are for learning what your novel or story is about.
Revision is working with that knowledge
to enlarge and enhance an idea, to re-form it.
Revision is one of the true pleasures of writing.

—BERNARD MALAMUD

It's safe to assume that everything you write for the entire length of your career will have to be rewritten.

Probably several times.

Finishing the first draft is the first stage. Deciding what needs to be fixed (and there will be stuff that needs to be fixed) is the second stage. Making the fixes is the third stage.

What do I mean by "fixes"?

One screenwriter's strengths are another's weaknesses. Every script has its own unique problems. The most common are as follows:

- It takes too long for the story to get started.
- It's unclear whose story it is.
- The dialogue is clunky.

- The main character isn't as interesting as the second lead.
- Too many scenes don't add anything to the story.
- A subplot goes off on a tangent that loses the thread of the main story.
- Transitions between some scenes don't make sense.
- A comedy is not funny enough (or not funny at all).
- The ending is unsatisfying.
- The script doesn't really end . . . it just stops and has loose ends that leave the audience scratching their heads.

In short, many different aspects of your screenplay might need to be fixed.

The purpose of the first draft is to get the story out of your head and onto the page to see what you've got, as well as what's missing.

If you're making your own movie you don't have to concern yourself with what agents, managers, producers, and studios think. You don't want or need their opinions. You only have to answer to yourself.

If you're smart, you should be your own toughest critic. Be a perfectionist.

When you're writing a short screenplay, approximately eight to fifteen pages, it's short enough for you to pore over not only every page but each line on every page, including dialogue and stage directions. Keep working on a scene until you get it down to the bone. Always remember: Less is more. Always cut and trim.

As you write more screenplays, you'll discover that there are three kinds of rewrites:

**The Page 1 Rewrite**: This rewrite means you basically start from scratch. It doesn't necessarily mean your first draft was horrible but that after getting it on paper you realized you needed to go in a different direction.

**The Grease and Lube**: Here you clarify or tighten dialogue, and add or eliminate scenes that don't quite work or aren't vital to the story.

**The Polish**: In this case you tighten, edit, and smooth over spots that aren't up to the level of the rest of the script.

If it's a comedy, you add jokes or make the jokes you've already got funnier.

Understand this: You might do three, four, or five drafts of your screenplay before you feel it's ready to be shot. By the final draft you will be satisfied and happy with it.

Be aware that when the time comes to shoot your screenplay, when it's on its feet and you're working with actors, you'll most likely rewrite it again, maybe not the whole script but parts of it.

Then, when it comes time to edit the film, you won't be rewriting, but you will most likely reshape it.

## Assignment

If your script went beyond ten pages you are an Overwriter.

If your script is under ten pages you are an Underwriter.

If your script is exactly ten pages you are someone who follows directions.

To look closely at your original screenplay don't read it off your monitor. Instead, print out the hard copy, hold it in your hands with a pen, and examine every line on each page.

If you went over ten pages, you will need to cut. If you went under, you'll need to write more.

Primarily what you should be looking for are spots that can be made better.

## Colloquium

# Making Your Short Screenplay: The Fear Before the Knowledge

The faster I write the better my output. If I'm going
slow I'm in trouble. It means I'm pushing the words
instead of being pulled by them.
—RAYMOND CHANDLER

Wanting to make a movie is a wonderful dream. Learning how to make that movie is an entirely different matter. It can be both an exciting and maddening experience.

It can also be scary.

I made a film (and I use the term loosely) when I was twenty-two with a Super 8 camera. It was a little over three minutes long. I cast my friends. I was the writer, director, producer, I acted in it, and I had a friend help me with the editing.

It was awful.

There was no plot to speak of. The camera work was jerky (and not on purpose like TV cop shows). I had no sense of how to frame a shot. I didn't have a shooting schedule. I shot most of it outdoors. By dumb luck the lighting was passable. The only halfway decent thing about the film was the editing that my friend did.

I wanted to go to film school. I wanted to be a filmmaker. But there were two things working against me: I had lousy grades and no money. My only experience with movies was *going* to them.

In hindsight, what turned me not off but *away* from pursuing a career as a filmmaker was the fact that I had no access to a film school. There were no how-to books available to help.

I would have to learn to do it myself, and that terrified me. I felt lost and inadequate and decided to channel my creative energies into becoming a playwright, which meant I didn't need any equipment. I could take playwriting classes and the only piece of equipment I needed was a typewriter.

What happened to me was that I had the fear before the knowledge.

By that I mean I was afraid of doing something simply because I assumed it would be difficult or problematic. But if we allow ourselves to bypass that feeling and go for it, we discover that it's not as frightening as we thought.

Have you ever been afraid to do something because you thought it would be dangerous or painful or mean certain failure? Some people won't fly. Some won't try new foods. Others are afraid to get out of a bad relationship or confront the jerk at work or at school whose relentless hassling drives them crazy.

Some screenwriters are afraid to direct their own films. This is a valid feeling, but it's another example of having the fear before the knowledge. How can I afford the equipment? How do I operate a camera? Where do I put the lights? How do I edit what I shoot? Who will show me how to do this stuff?

When you're attending a university film school these worries are no longer problems because you have access to equipment: cameras, lights, dollies, recording and editing devices, the whole nine yards, and can use stuff that otherwise would cost big bucks to buy or rent, and you also have access to teachers who are working in their respective fields. This combination makes for a terrific learning environment.

People who don't go to film school can learn how to write, direct, edit, and produce films, too. You have to make do with less, but your work can be just as creative and imaginative.

Because you're a beginning filmmaker with presumably not a lot of cash to spend, I want you to make your first movies as inexpensively as possible.

You'll be shooting on video.

Once you've picked up the basics you can move up to the costlier, more cream-of-the-crop software and on to making movies that are shot on film.

For now, I'm going to point you in the direction of iMovie, which is already installed for free on all Mac computers of recent years, or similar software available for Windows. It'll enable you to do all the basic editing you'll need to make a short film without the heavy extra cost and the dramatic learning curve of programs like Final Cut and Pro Tools (which in my opinion can be too intimidating for novice filmmakers).

Making a film, no matter how short, is a challenge. In these pages I'll point you in the direction of the least intimidating, most rewarding route of gratification that will take you to a final product you can show people and feel pleased about.

The beauty of today's computer world is that anyone who buys a Mac and any discerning person who buys a computer running a Windows operating system can edit videos right away without manuals or pricey software. There are limitations with iMovie, but they won't get in the way of talent.

Realize that limitations can breed creativity. The limitations I'm talking about are that perhaps you won't have superglitzy fancy title sequences or fluid dissolves. But these options are better left off anyway, because beginners often overuse them to cover up a weak story.

In the techie world, there is a widely known, comically named behavior that takes over many a novice when they get into technology-related arts.

It's said they get GAS–*Gear Acquisition Syndrome.*

The inexperienced think the more they buy, the more advanced the technology they have, the more amazing their work will be.

It doesn't work that way.

More gadgets and gizmos usually become a huge distraction. Novices may try to "buy" a sense of artistic accomplishment by getting all the glitzy stuff available to them, but it seldom works, because art is *never* about the technology.

A creative person with a three-hundred-dollar consumer-level mini-DV (digital video) camera and free software such as iMovie can create more exhilarating work than someone with a better DV camera at ten times the price and software that costs a grand.

The less creative person without a solid foundation of screenwriting skills who spent five thousand dollars on technology will be deficient, and his stuff will look amateurish. Any production company or agent won't care what his film looks like from a production quality standpoint. They will look for the raw talent and whether it's there or not. Fortunately, talent is not a function of money.

Bottom line: Making a movie is easier and cheaper than ever before.

In the next part of this book I'm going to give you a crash course in making a short film. Everything you learn will be practice for making your full-length feature film.

By now you've written and rewritten a short screenplay, so you have the script. Because you're going to direct it, you don't have to waste time looking for a director.

You're also probably going to operate the camera.

By now, you've also managed to find a few friends who will help you out in various ways. So you have a cast and crew.

What comes next is making the movie.

Welcome to showbiz.

# Part III

# Filmmaking

For Filmmakers and Screenwriters Who Never
Thought About Making Their Own Movie

Go see it and see for yourself why
you shouldn't see it.
–SAMUEL GOLDWYN

## Lecture 7

# Stuff You Need to Know About Making Your Screenplay, Whether It's 8 Pages or 108 Pages

You can't wait for inspiration.
You have to go after it with a club.
—JACK LONDON

The first movie you make will be bad. Whether or not you have a solid story line, it'll probably *look* bad. It'll be either underlit or overlit. It will sound bad in certain sections. Maybe you'll be able to hear the actors, but chances are you'll also hear the local traffic or that low-flying plane or even the refrigerator in that long kitchen sequence.

The acting will most likely be bad because you used your friends or relatives or maybe even yourself. If you did manage to cast actors who had some experience in high school plays, odds are they'll be bad because they haven't acted in a film and you're new to directing or you didn't know how to "direct" them because maybe you were too nice or too mean or too unfocused. (More about casting in the next lecture.)

You'll realize that you placed the camera in the wrong place a number of times. You'll realize that you should've done another take on a few shots that you were convinced worked. You took too long on several of your outdoor shots and the weather changed, so the glorious sunny day when you began your picnic scene turned into a morose, cloudy day.

In short, you'll have a bunch of scenes, some that work and some that don't work. You'll try to edit them in a way that will make sense and depends on how good an editor you are (considering that it's your first film, you'll probably be mediocre). No matter the relative merits of your film, there is one big victory in this scenario: You've completed a film.

Just as you completed the screenplay, got some feedback from people whose opinion you respected, did a few drafts and a polish, when you shot the script maybe you did some improvising during the shoot or some last-minute rewrites or you got an idea for a new pivotal plot point and wound up with a pretty good batch of usable film.

As you look at what you've shot, you'll go through an editing process similar to what you did with your screenplay. You'll realize the mistakes you made with the lighting, sound, casting, camera angles, and crew, and once you've tried to pull everything together in the editing and mixing, you'll already be better and more accomplished than when you started.

This is the beauty and wonder of experience.

You'll do better the next time.

And the more next times you have, the more you'll continue to grow and develop as a filmmaker.

When you do better on your next screenplay, you'll have a story that's perhaps more shootable.

Fewer actors.

Fewer sets.

Less talk.

You'll plan the way you shoot the movie better.

You'll have scenes that help to tell the story rather than serving to indulge your ego.

Your characters will be more rounded and three-dimensional.

Bottom line: The only way to learn how to write a script is to write one. The only way to learn how to direct a movie is to direct one.

What follows are the six most important things you need to know about making your movie:

1. Get the script as tight as can be. This means rewriting and rethinking and revising and polishing until you feel the script is ready to go. You'll instinctively feel it's ready. You've gotten feedback from your one or two trusted friends and you'll have a gut sense that no more constructive work can be done at your computer.

2. Understand that although your script may seem ready to go, it isn't. It's good enough to show to people, specifically the people you want to help you make it. Let's assume you're starting with a five-minute short. Let's also assume your budget is small—say under three hundred dollars. Let's go even cheaper. Many former students of mine feel that no first-time filmmakers should spend more than fifty dollars on their first short if they're shooting on video. Two hours for one tape at about five dollars per tape.

   When you shoot on film it's more expensive, but if you're frugal and have the right material you can get away with a tiny budget. A former student of mine shot a three-minute short on real 16mm film for two hundred dollars. He entered it in HBO's Project Greenlight (see Resources section) and made it into the Top 50, beating out seventeen hundred filmmakers. But as I said, learn how to shoot on video before moving on to film.

   Obviously you could spend more if you rented lighting or did something fancy or shot on real film or if you paid actors and bought them food. We're operating under the assumption that money is an issue. You may not be flat broke, but you're watching your pennies. Point is: A lot can be done with a little money.

3. If you're using your own money, don't worry about what anybody thinks. Not only are you the writer and director; you're also the producer. You're the boss. If you asked your father and uncle for money, even though they presumably had never read a screenplay in their lives they would want to read yours and if they didn't get it or they found certain things objectionable, they'd have to be listened to. But let's assume you're using your own money.

4. Get help. In film school there are plenty of people around to pitch in. There are courses designed to put a small group of people together to act as a crew for one another's movies. But because you're not in film school or a film program, you won't have easy access to people who can help you. And the people you *do* have access to may not know anything about shooting a film.

5. Teach whoever is helping you. Who will you need? You may need a camera operator. Maybe not. Maybe you're going to do that, too. You'll need somebody to help you with the lighting. You'll need someone to take care of the sound. You'll need help auditioning actors, and before you audition them you'll need to spread the word that you're making a film. In New York, film students from NYU, to Columbia, to the New York Film Academy, to the School of Visual Arts place ads in *Back Stage* (see Resources section). If you live in Idaho you may not have that kind of access to a talent pool. But you have access to high school drama clubs, community theaters, college drama departments. However you do it, you'll need help casting your movie. Don't be afraid to ask for help or call in favors. Lots of student filmmakers also use craigslist.com to find actors and crew.

6. Develop a preproduction, production, and postproduction schedule. Preproduction is what you do before you make your movie. Because you're directing your own screenplay, preproduction starts the day the script is ready. It involves finding the money to finance the project, getting equipment and a crew, selecting locations, casting, and creating your shot list. The production part is when you're shooting the film. Postproduction is mostly editing and applying sound effects and music and rerecording dialogue if necessary.

## Some Thoughts on Feedback

Listen to what people have to say, but make sure you show your script to the *right* people. Family members should be avoided. They will either like it too much or hate it too much. Same with wives, husbands, boyfriends, and girlfriends. They'll like it too much or hate it too much. What you want is someone who will be honest. Someone you can trust not to bullshit you. Someone who can tell you what works and, more important, what doesn't work. Someone who will give you feedback on what *you* wrote, not the movie he would write. If you're lucky, you'll find one or two people like this. Despite what I just said, you might be fortunate enough to have a sibling or spouse who will fit the bill. But probably not. People who have some experience with filmmaking or reading scripts are particularly valuable since they have a standard against which to compare your work. You might find an honest sister, but that doesn't mean her honesty is going to be of much use if she doesn't know what she's talking about.

# Lecture 8

# Directing the Actor

When an actor comes to me and wants to discuss his character,
I say, "It's in the script." If he says, "But what's my motivation?"
I say, "Your salary."
—ALFRED HITCHCOCK

What does a director do? At its most basic level, directing is telling people what to do. There's a right way to approach this and a wrong way. Being demanding is the right way for some. Being warm and fuzzy gets results for others.

You have to find your style, but most likely you won't know what that style is until you start shooting your film. First and foremost, be strong. Be a leader. Don't be afraid to be confrontational. If there are actors who are giving you crap, call them on it. Don't be too forgiving if someone on your crew isn't cutting it. Better to have someone else make up the slack than to have one jerk who's not pulling his weight. Don't hope for problems to correct themselves. They won't. It's up to you to fix whatever's not going well. And by doing so you'll gain the respect of the people you're working with.

However, if you're a control freak (and I mean that in a good way), you're operating at an advantage, provided you have people skills. If you don't have people skills, you're operating at a disadvantage and need to learn them. What are people skills? If you have to ask, you don't have them. Let's say they mean the ability to talk to other human beings in a civil, respectful manner.

On the other hand, if you're sensitive, soft-spoken, considerate of the feelings of others, and not particularly bossy or aggressive, you'll need to learn how to assert yourself to solidify your position as the person in charge.

A good director knows how to talk to actors. Equally important is being able to listen to them. Some actors will ask a million questions. Others won't ask one. Some will challenge you. Others will do what you ask. You must adapt to each personality.

As a director you should have a respect for and understanding of the actors' craft. If you've never acted yourself, try it. You'll see acting from an entirely different perspective.

Acting isn't just memorizing lines; it's understanding what the lines mean and interpreting them. A smart director knows that some actors show up with the scene nailed while others need time to find their way. Certain actors need lots of rehearsal and numerous takes. Others hate rehearsing because they think it hinders spontaneity and dislike doing more than one or two takes. You have to deal with these differences, especially as you move up the food chain from a director of a five-minute short to a hotshot Hollywood director.

Directing your cousin Waldo and the cute girl from your local community theater who was so convincing as Tzeitel in their summer production of *Fiddler on the Roof* will be different from directing two stars.

The job of the director is to make sure the performances serve the material. Because it's *your* screenplay, it's your material. You're going to want the best people acting in your movie that you can possibly get.

## How Do You Know If an Actor's Any Good?

You can get a head start on knowing how an actor might be to work with during auditions. An audition is essentially a job interview.

When a regular person goes on a job interview she's on her best behavior. She's primed to behave in a way that she assumes the inter-
viewer wants her to behave.

Auditions are no different.

An actor wants a part, even if it's a crappy part in a crappy film. He
wants the experience and he needs the credit on his résumé. Getting
a real credit is important. Unless he's self-destructive or unusually
confident, he'll be on his best behavior. Chatty. Smiley. Friendly. He'll
probably come prepared with a monologue or some other type of audition piece. Maybe there will be a scene from your screenplay that
you ask him to read.

Maybe he'll do pretty good.

Maybe very good.

Maybe brilliantly and you'll want to hire him on the spot.

Be careful. An incredible audition doesn't necessarily mean he'll
deliver the performance you want during the shoot.

There's an understanding in film, TV, and theater that some actors
give great auditions and go steadily downhill after that. Other actors
give abysmal auditions but get consistently better. Until you've worked
with a particular actor or you know someone who has, you never
know what you're getting.

Here's a little trick to help you see what you've got.

Give the guy who gives an amazing audition a direction. Tell him to
do whatever he did that was so good in a different way. Tell him to
play it with a Southern accent. Tell him to play it gay. Tell him to play it
as if he's angry. Or sad. Or anything.

If he does what you've asked him to do, it means he can take direction. If he doesn't, it means he can't. That's a dangerous person to
hire. You want an actor who will listen to you.

On the other side of the coin, you also want an actor who's creative and who has ideas. You want an actor who is interested in making the scene work—in making the *movie* work. An actor who will

listen to you if you have good ideas and expect you to listen to him if *he* has good ideas.

You may have a clear plan in your head how you're going to shoot a scene. You may have it storyboarded (more about that in a bit). You may have played it out in your head a dozen times.

But when you show up on the set, if one of the actors offers a suggestion that will make the scene work and look better, be flexible enough to take it. This is not to say that every actor will have amazing ideas for every scene. Many times an actor will have bad ideas or suggestions that are just wrong or stupid.

But if you create an atmosphere of collaboration on your set, you may get lucky and have an actor come up with something that you never thought of. It'll make you and the finished product better. However, beware the opinions of too many people. Some will have crazy ideas or suggestions that are totally wrong. Trust who you feel you can, but follow your own vision.

Getting the best actors you can possibly find is your uppermost goal. However, depending on where you live and the talent pool you're drawing from, you may not get a cast that's first-rate (or even third-rate). You might get one really terrific actor, one decent one, and the rest pretty bad.

Which brings us to another problem you'll face.

Is it better to have an actor who can act but is physically wrong for the part or an actor with less talent who is physically right?

For example, the lead part in your movie is a gorgeous, sexy twenty-three-year-old babe who works in an office. All the guys she works with drool over her. And let's say there's an important scene with a big payoff having to do with how attractive and desirable the woman is.

Do you cast a gorgeous actress with limited abilities or do you cast a woman who's forty pounds overweight, plain, and not very attractive but is a *wonderful* actress?

What do you do?

My advice is to go with the gorgeous actress with lesser abilities. Why? Because that's what the script called for. A woman *desired* by her coworkers.

No matter how brilliant the overweight, unattractive actress might be in the role, by virtue of her physical appearance she would not serve the material. You don't want your audience looking at the unattractive performer wondering why all the guys she works with desire her.

Just as casting a sexy blonde in the part of a plain Jane wouldn't serve *that* material.

A playwright friend of mine experienced this exact dilemma. At the insistence of the director he agreed to cast a talented women ten years older and seventy pounds heavier than the part of the sexy, desirable babe his play called for. I saw the production. All I kept wondering was, *Why are all the men in the play so horny for this woman?* Granted, she was very good as an actress.

But she was wrong for the part and casting her diminished the strength of the play.

Most likely, when you shoot your short screenplay you will have to make do with the pool of actors available to you.

Cast as well as you possibly can. Don't overrehearse, but give the actors a chance to get to know you, the material, and one another. You're building a temporary family that needs to work together.

Your next test will be to see how *you* measure up as a director.

# Lecture 9

# Filmmaking Pitfalls

Being a writer is like having homework
every night for the rest of your life.
–LAWRENCE KASDAN

## Seven First Timer Mistakes

### 1: Not Taking Enough Shots

You hear how Stanley Kubrick would shoot an endless number of takes on a scene. And I mean endless. Ten, twenty, forty. More. You also hear how other directors only shoot one or two takes. Clint Eastwood comes to mind.

I'm not saying that Kubrick was wrong or that Eastwood is right. The number of takes is a matter of experience and personal style. Big-time directors are also working with more experienced actors, yet why do some directors keep asking for more takes and others don't? Many directors like to have numerous choices during the editing process. Others prefer to have only two or three takes from which to choose. Again, it's a matter of personal style. Or budget. Certain successful directors are consistently hired because they are known for always coming in on budget (or even under budget). Others get work because they have reputations for being "actors' directors," which means that they have a certain manner that actors love. Bottom line: If you like a lot of takes and you've got the money, shoot away.

You're shooting on video, which is cheap compared to shooting on film. Most likely you'll be using your relatives or some kids from your high school alma mater drama club, which means you might not be in a position to rely on the acting ability of your cast. Even so, doing lots and lots of takes can be debilitating to your cast. And it's not a good practice for first-time directors to get too crazy searching for the perfect take.

This being said, you'd be wise to get in the habit of doing as reasonable a number of additional shots as your time and budget allow. This is where a storyboard comes in handy.

## 2: Not Using a Storyboard

Don't ever shoot anything without having done a storyboard first. A storyboard is a series of sketches (resembling a cartoon strip) showing how each shot is to be filmed. Storyboards, in the common production sense, are not for improvising but are more of a strict blueprint. You can use one sheet of typing paper and divide it into six shots. You don't have to be a great artist to do a storyboard. Rough sketches are enough. I have a filmmaker friend who uses stick figures. All you need is something to hold in your hands that indicates which shots you're going to do.

If you're shooting a close-up of three pancakes in a frying pan, draw a circle to represent the pan and three smaller circles in the pan to represent the pancakes.

## 3: Not Doing Enough Camera Setups

The maxim "You only get one chance to make a first impression" is applicable to filmmaking. However, there will be times when you only get one chance to make the shot you want (the weather's bad; your actor has to leave early or shows up with a sore throat). If that's the case, you have no choice but to get it right the first time.

However, if you're using your aunt Sally's kitchen for that crucial breakfast scene and she doesn't mind you and your crew being there, take advantage of her generosity. After you've gotten your master shot and the close-ups you planned for, take a few more. Do a setup from a different angle or two.

Make sure you've got *coverage.*

Coverage is an indeterminate number of more detailed shots that are intended to be intercut with a master shot or scene.

Coverage is key to seeing a scene all the way through. You can use lines and actions taken from all the shots and angles you choose to deliver your story with dramatic visual effect.

Because you're in a kitchen, take advantage of "place" and get some extra shots of a whistling teakettle or coffee beans being ground or a knife being sharpened to fill out your scene. These are called *cutaways.* You might never use them, but you'll have them for later when you're cutting the kitchen scene together.

Having some extra shots on hand covers you in case of an emergency. Follow this basic rule: In filmmaking it's better to have too many scenes to choose from than not enough. Use different angles and have a diversity of shots.

Aunt Sally has promised you one day and one day only in her kitchen, so be as creative as you possibly can that day.

You don't have to go crazy and be Robert Altman, but get the shots while you can.

## 4: Not Thinking Like Alfred Hitchcock

Alfred Hitchcock wasn't a writer, but the scripts of his films were his first priority. He knew that without a taut script that he had personally pored over line by line, he wasn't ready to start production. He hired people to write his screenplays, many of them upper-echelon screenwriters of their day such as Ernest Lehman (*North by Northwest*). Undoubtedly Hitchcock worked closely with them. He is famous for having the entire movie shot in his head scene by scene. When he showed up on the set he knew what he wanted and that was that.

"What about spontaneity?" you might ask. "What if I meticulously planned something and then in the middle of the shoot I get an idea for something else?"

If you do, cool. Definitely shoot it. But as a beginning filmmaker with a tiny budget, limited time, probably not the best actors, an inexperienced crew, and little experience directing, you should concentrate on the game plan you've already established.

It's like when you're on a vacation and you're driving from New York to the Grand Canyon. You're taking a ten-day trip and you have seven places you want to visit. Your money and time are tightly budgeted. You've planned everything down to the penny. There's no room for veering off course. If you do, it might be interesting, but you risk disrupting the itinerary you spent weeks saving and working for.

## 5: Not Being Smart About Lighting and Sound

Two aspects of the filmmaking process that should *not* be underestimated are lighting and sound. I can't emphasize enough the number of dark, grainy, underlit films I've sat through. Even worse are those with sound so bad they seem as if they were recorded on a twenty-dollar tape recorder. (The exception to the rule is Robert Rodriguez, who shot his first feature film with a regular tape recorder and household lamps.)

If your film isn't properly lit, all the solid acting, clever dialogue, and compelling storytelling will be lost because your audience won't be able to *see* it.

A newspaper photographer friend says that when it comes to taking pictures, "it's not the camera; it's the photographer."

You can have a great camera, but if you don't know how to frame a shot and take distance into account, and if you can't gauge the amount of natural light or lack of practical lighting if you're inside, you're going to take a lousy picture.

Like so many of the skills required to make a movie, lighting is eminently learnable (and, arguably, the most challenging craft in filmmak-

There are three basic lights: Key Light, Fill Light, and Back Light. All other lights are for effect or to mimic the lighting of a real setting as best as possible.

**Key Light** is the main light that makes your subject viewable.

**Fill Light** is used on the other (front) side of the subject so that he/she/it doesn't have one side/half in strong shadow or darkness. Fill Light is not usually as strong as the Key Light.

**Back Light** is a light behind and pointing at the subject, which serves to offer a little separation between the subject and the background so he/she/it doesn't blend in and away with a wall or sky, and so forth. If you look at the classic films of the thirties and forties featuring women stars, you can often see the distinct contour and outline of their hair set against the rest of the room behind them. A Back Light does this. Remember that lighting is also creative and improvisational, so you don't necessarily need to use all three types of lighting in every shot.

ing by far). Again, by doing it and doing it badly, you'll learn the hard way how to get it right. Once you've mastered the fundamentals, then it's time to explore the greater heights and possibilities of lighting.

Let's say that down the road in your career you're directing a suspense thriller for Paramount. You won't want bold and brassy pastels to convey terror. If you're doing a sexy seduction scene, you'll want the lighting to illustrate the romance and passion. If you want to show that your main character is depressed and antisocial and hasn't paid her electric bill in four months and lives in a dingy, neglected tenement, lighting will work hand in hand with the set designer to get the tone across.

Sound is also instrumental in conveying mood and atmosphere.

There are reasons why there are Academy Awards for Sound. Most new screenwriters, dare I say all screenwriters, no matter what their experience, never give much thought to sound while writing their scripts.

If you're making a film, suddenly sound takes on a whole new importance. While story is 99 percent of a movie, sound is 50 percent of the moviegoing experience.

Whether you're making a short or you've raised enough money to make a full-length film, odds are your cast is minimal and so are your locations. Maybe at least half of your scenes will take place outside, where it's difficult to control your environment because of the sounds of life all around you.

When shooting on location, take advantage of ambient sounds. These are the natural sounds germane to the locale. If you're shooting at a swimming pool, there's the sound of someone diving into the water. Not only the splash but also the noise of the diving board bouncing. If you're shooting on a beach, you can get the sound of waves crashing. If you're shooting on a bridge overlooking a freeway, record the sounds of the cars whizzing by below.

These sounds can be captured by using inexpensive consumer equipment, provided you make sure to place the microphone in the right place. For sound effects—sounds recorded separately and added during the editing—place the microphone extremely close to the sound source to remove the sounds in the background. Always grab room tone or location sounds: thirty seconds of ambience so later on you can have an ambient track to simulate the setting. These sounds are recorded without the camera running.

Room tone is usually recorded not so much to simulate setting but rather to cover the chops that occur from cutting dialogue. The sounds of setting, in bigger-budget pictures, are often created from scratch.

Here's a trick offered by my friend the filmmaker Andrew Stoeckley: "Regardless of what you're recording for what purpose, always keep the record level of the tape machine *the same* throughout the entire production. Why? Because when you mix the sounds later during editing they will all have approximately the same level of 'hiss' and will blend nicely. Otherwise, a two-second effect, like a door slamming or water droplet, et cetera, may come in and stick out solely because of the sudden increase in hiss, if its record level was cranked up."

By "hiss" Andrew is referring to the level of ambient sound, air, in the room, which always gets recorded, even though most novices don't think about it. When you turn up the mic level you are also turning up the sound of air.

Guess what?

By the time you've finished shooting your first couple of short films, getting the proper sound level will be second nature to you as you move onward and upward in your development.

If you're shooting indoors in a house or apartment, turn off the refrigerator. The slightest noise can screw up that difficult, talky scene that serves as the turning point of your film.

If there's a scene in your script that indicates an extreme close-up on a shower nozzle as a droplet of water comes out and plops into the bathtub, the sound of that droplet landing can enhance the tone of the scene.

As a director, view lighting and sound as two key allies in making your film. And as with all skills, the best way to learn is by doing.

---

There are film school courses devoted *entirely* to these skills, as well as a number of excellent books on both subjects. Check out *Film Lighting: Talks with Hollywood's Cinematographers and Gaffers* by Kris Malkiewicz. And for sound: *Sound Design: The Expressive Power of Music, Voice, and Sound Effects in Cinema* by David Sonnenschein.

## 6: Not Having a Clear Vision in Your Head

Don't show up on the set without knowing what you're going to shoot that day. Be prepared. When you go to sleep the night before you should have a shot list, so when you wake up you're not arbitrarily deciding what you're going to do and where you're going to put the camera. A shot list is the schedule of camera angles and setups.

A director *lives* with his shot list. It also helps to have a line script (the pages of the script you're going to shoot each day) so you can follow along and make sure you've covered every line in the screenplay through the various shots you took for each scene. You want to avoid missing one line from a scene so you're forced to cut it or reshoot.

Having lists and planning ahead seems like a no-brainer. What kind of filmmaker would show up not quite sure what he's going to do that day? (Exception to the rule: Woody Allen, who says that 99 percent of the time, he shows up on set with no idea where he's going to place the camera. That's Woody for ya!) Others can't do their prep work because human nature being what it is, there are some of us who study for tests and some of us who don't. Even if we haven't studied for the big test, we still show up and hope we'll guess right.

Screenwriters are like that, too. If you're in a screenwriting class and you have ten pages to do, you can spend a week working on them, revising and polishing, or you can dash them out a couple of hours (or twenty minutes) before class.

Why should filmmaking be any different? Your heart may be in the right place, but if you stay out late with your new girlfriend or partying with your buds, the next day you're going to show up on *your* set with only a vague idea (if you're lucky) of what you're going to do that day.

This is bad because you lose time, money, and the respect of your crew and actors. Since they're all probably working for free and are looking to you for guidance, holding on to their respect (and giving them respect by planning ahead) is crucial to getting the film done.

Respect generates loyalty. If your cast and crew see you show up every day focused and knowing exactly what you're going to do, you make them feel safe. Actors like to feel safe to be able to give you their best performance.

Remember, making a film is basically following the leader and *you're* the leader. You set the tone and mood on the set.

## 7: Not Having a Respect for and Understanding of Editing

After a movie with big stars, a celebrated director, and a respected writer bombs, the excuses begin. They say they knew the script was weak, but they had a shooting schedule to maintain so they figured they'd fix it in the rehearsal.

Rehearsal came and went and the script still wasn't right, so they figured they'd fix it on the set with some last-minute rewriting and maybe some improvisation from the star.

The shoot is over, but the director knows that the rewrites and improvs didn't do the trick. He says he'll fix it in the editing. Even then there are problems.

The director had the right idea. Editing is the stage of filmmaking when mistakes are fixed. Of course, editing is more than that. It's the final step in the telling of your story.

You write a scene a certain way. Then you shoot the scene with a number of setups and angles and half-a-dozen close-ups.

Then you get into the editing room and piece together all the takes in a cohesive manner that enables you to tell the story.

You realize that some scenes can be edited down or eliminated completely. Maybe you find some neat shot that happened by accident and brings new life to a problematic scene. Maybe you decide to use a voice-over to cover up a badly lit scene. If you've got enough time, money, and people, maybe you can reshoot a few scenes.

Basically, you'll do an inventory of the material you can and can't use and get to work. The editing process will help you refine your sto-

Book Recommendation: *In the Blink of an Eye: A Perspective on Film Editing*, revised second edition, by Walter Murch.

rytelling skills. You'll learn what is absolutely necessary and what isn't. Some directors watch all the footage after the shoot and write down which shots they liked best. This saves time in the editing room.

At this stage of your career you'll most likely be editing your film yourself. However, as your career progresses, like most successful directors, you'll work with a professional editor. When you arrive at this point your relationship with an editor will be give-and-take. You'll like some shots. He'll say others work better and give his reasons why. You'll go back and forth. It's part of the process.

But for now, plan on editing your film yourself. And approach it as the final step in the process of realizing your vision as screenwriter and director.

**Lecture 10**

# Lights! Camera! Action! Editing!

Write the story, take out all the
good lines, and see if it works.
—ERNEST HEMINGWAY

Because I want you to shoot on video I won't spend time discussing the techniques of 16mm film cinematography. That isn't teachable in a book. I won't get into the use of light meters, either, since they're not used in video production for the most part and it's impossible to adequately teach lighting through a book.

It's also beyond the scope here to outline specific details about video-editing software, but some general information will be useful for you as you're starting out.

Basically, the raw footage that you shoot needs to exist on mini-DV tape before computer editing can begin. If you're shooting video, it'll already be on mini-DV tape unless you're using an obsolete technology like VHS or Hi-8, in which case you need to dub it from a VCR to a mini-DV camcorder. If you use these older formats, the quality will suffer significantly.

Ideally, the camera you use should be mini-DV. Prices can range from three hundred to three thousand dollars. The advantages of the more expensive camera are:

- Better lens and possible ability to interchange lenses.
- Better color, better resolution.
- On some cameras, the ability to shoot the video at twenty-four frames per second rather than the standard thirty; thus the motion looks more like it does on film.
- More control over exposure and a faster and more accurate built-in light meter.
- Making you look cooler to passersby.

## A Big However

A three-hundred-dollar mini-DV camera is just fine for your purposes now.

If you're shooting on film, you'll need to have the lab transfer the processed footage to mini-DV and you must still own or have access to at least a cheap mini-DV camcorder so the footage can be dumped into the computer.

Your computer must have a "Firewire" or "IEEE1394" port (two names for the same thing). On most computers today, these ports are standard. On older computers, they might have to be added, for usually less than a hundred dollars.

The camera connects to the computer with a Firewire/IEEE1394 cable, and the software, whether it's iMovie, Final Cut, Vegas (for Windows), or any of the dozens of others, will have a feature that downloads the video from the camera into the computer, called capturing.

If you're new to editing software, you'll find that iMovie is straightforward enough to follow. You'll be able to figure out how it works in no time at all. Remember, iMovie was designed for the average layperson to use. (If you already have or choose to use more advanced software, the manual will explain the specifics of that particular program.)

## Your Hard Drive

You also need to know that video takes up a lot of hard-drive space. You'll need approximately 250 MB of space for every one minute of footage. That adds up really fast. Most newer computers come with hard drives of at least 40 GB, so that should be enough for a couple of short films (under thirty minutes), maybe more.

The actual amount that gets used in the end is dependent on how long the film is and how much footage was shot to arrive at the final edit. Some will shoot very tightly, with a ratio of about 2- or 3-to-1, while others might shoot at 10-to-1. (The ratio refers to the amount of footage shot versus final length of film. A ten-minute film with an hour of raw footage has a 6-to-1 shooting ratio.)

If you really get into making short films it would be good to eventually get a second hard drive for use exclusively for the video data. Hard drives aren't that expensive now, and a video-editing system actually runs a lot smoother when the software and video data aren't running off the same drive. And it will give you more drive space for more projects.

A secondary hard drive can be connected in a variety of ways today. Many people use Firewire drives that plug into the computer just like the camera. This makes the drives portable, which can also be an advantage.

Another most effective and convenient way to connect a second hard drive externally is to use USB, but both the computer and the drive must support USB 2.0, which is an upgraded standard to the original USB and has the transfer speeds necessary for working with video and audio. If either device uses only USB 1, then it will not function effectively.

The most effective way to have a second hard drive is to add it internally into a spare drive bay within the computer. Another option for internal or external drive additions is to use the SCSI format, but this requires adding a SCSI port to your computer, and SCSI hardware, including drives, is more expensive and harder to configure.

## Editing

All editing programs do basically the same thing. They present you with long strips of video—raw footage—and let you chop the strips up and move the pieces around on a "time line." They have an extra couple of audio tracks for laying down music or effects (in addition to the automatic audio track that's included on the video clips) or, in the case of Vegas, have an unlimited number of audio tracks available.

## Sound Effects

If you've recorded sound effects you'll have to get those sounds into your computer, too. This process varies widely, depending on which sound-recording technology you use (and there are many). Staying with my theme of keeping things simple and inexpensive, I recommend that you use your video camera and maybe an external mic to get these sounds and record them directly to a mini-DV tape (one that's not also being used for video, obviously).

This way you can dump the tape into the computer just like the video and the sound will be there as part of a dummy video clip. This is just one option.

Most computers have a microphone jack. You can connect it to your tape recorder, DAT machine, or whatever else you have and record into the computer that way. However, the quality may suffer, as many computer sound cards are not of particularly high quality (although some are).

Once you get everything onto your computer you'll move the images and sounds along the time line until your edit is complete. At this point the software can spit it back out to the mini-DV camera along the same cable. Of course, you should have a *blank* mini-DV tape in the camera to receive it.

Now your project is complete, on mini-DV tape. When you show it to friends and family in-person you should show it off the DV camera connected to a TV, because the resolution is about twice that of VHS. Or you can easily dub from the camera to a VHS VCR and pass around copies that way. Most newer computers come with DVD-R drives, so instead of dumping the finished project back out to tape, you can burn it onto DVD instead.

## Some Final Thoughts Before You Start Shooting

As I said earlier with regard to lighting, make sure there *is* light. Even if it's a dark scene, make sure there's light of some kind on whatever is in the scene that's important for us to see. With video you have the advantage of trial and error.

Many first-time filmmakers think making a film is about being on the set and getting the shots. They often put all their hard work and concentration into this aspect. They don't understand that *editing* is where the film actually gets made. In fact, many directors consider editing the best part of filmmaking. Editing is also where the filmmaker is most vulnerable to showing whether or not he has taste and talent. Not to mention standards. Completely crappy footage, if edited together well, is always better than great footage edited badly.

Incidentally, the DVD *Visions of Light: The Art of Cinematography* is worth watching. This is a fascinating documentary about lighting and very inspiring. Cameramen and -women discuss the craft and art of cinematography and of the DP (the director of photography), illustrating their points with clips from one hundred films, from *The Birth of a Nation* to *Do the Right Thing*.

Don't rush the editing process. Take the time to put all the pieces of your film together.

Okay. You've got your revised short screenplay that has a nifty story. You've done a storyboard. You'll need a mini-DV camcorder and a few tapes. You'll need to audition some actors and pick your locations. You'll need a few loyal friends to help you. Make sure you have enough light. Get your shot list ready for each day's shooting.

Now go make your movie.

# When You're Ready to Shoot on Film

First and foremost, it's important to understand that shooting on film is more expensive, more difficult, and more time-consuming and requires greater patience throughout the process than shooting on video. Unlike video, you won't know if your takes were successful until after you've spent a lot of money at a lab and got the footage back.

Also unlike video, you can't rely on trial and error as much or freely shoot whatever you'd like, as much as you'd like, because each second that film passes through the camera, your cost is going up. You also can't rewind and record over it.

In addition, the camera equipment is expensive to buy, expensive to rent, and difficult to find if you want to borrow it for free. Film is also vulnerable to errors that can be discouraging and costly—it might jam in the camera if not loaded correctly or the camera might have light leaks that streak your footage with lines of white.

## The Demands on Lighting Are Greater

Unlike video, you must carefully measure the light levels in every shot before you roll the camera, using a light meter. If you shoot outside, the sudden movement of a cloud in front of the sun just before you shoot can throw off the exposure significantly if you don't adjust accordingly or wait for the cloud to move. With video cameras, adjustments to changes in light are automatically made by the internal light meter of the camera. *This does not happen with film.*

Also when you shoot on film, the sound is not recorded onto the film as it is with video. You must record the sound separately and sync it up later. This is one of the primary reasons slate boards (aka clappers) are used. When the clap comes down, it offers both visual and aural cues that are aligned later so the rest of the scene and its dialogue sync up with the actor's moving lips.

Matching visual and audio later is either very time-consuming if you do it yourself (done in the computer by moving the sound takes around the time line to match them up with the images) or expensive if you choose to have the lab do this for you when it develops your footage. (Having the lab do it requires that during production, all of your sound takes are also carefully logged on paper and are handed to the lab with the sound tapes, which also must be very organized.)

Film also requires that you have at least two or three crew members dedicated to sound during the production: one to operate the sound recorder (today this is often a DAT machine, which is in and of itself an expensive item to buy or rent), one to hold the microphone (on a boom pole)—the "boom operator," and another to clap the slate board at the beginning of each take.

You can't rely on cheap tape recorders to record your dialogue because they don't run at what is called crystal sync, which means operating at a strict speed that never wavers. If the sound recording increases or decreases in speed slightly, it may not be audible to you but will be very noticeable when you sync the sound up later with film and notice that sometimes the actors' lips are not matching up with their words.

So you need to use a DAT machine, CD recorder, or something digital. Nagra reel-to-reel tape recorders, which run at crystal sync, used to be an industry standard (currently they're still used in many film schools). But they are large, costly machines, and in today's world they offer no practical advantages over digital recording.

You could use a mini-DV camcorder as your sound recorder, plugging the mic into it as mentioned earlier in this book, if you want to save money. It would be easy to download the sound into your computer this way, too. (Remember this tip: Keep the lens cap on if you use this approach so you don't confuse your sound takes with your video takes after it's all in the computer. You'll have plenty of video takes to keep track of already without cluttering up the confusion with video that you definitely won't use.)

Otherwise you have to spend hours recording your dialogue into the computer via its sound card, which is, however, usually how it's done. A DAT machine is usually going to get you better sound than a camcorder anyway.

## Finally, the Costs

There are many different formats for shooting film. Most people start out with 16mm, which is much less expensive than 35mm. The raw footage for 16mm costs anywhere from $0.20 per foot to $0.35. One foot of 16mm contains forty frames and there are twenty-four frames in a second, so this equates to approximately $7 to $13 per minute of *raw footage.*

Remember that a final film of five minutes will usually have at least ten to thirty minutes of raw footage. Even if you shot just one take for each shot, you still have all the slack at the beginning of each take when the slate board is clapped and slack at the end after you yell, "Cut!"

You still have to pay a lab to process the footage and transfer it to mini-DV tape so you can edit it digitally in your computer. Lab costs widely vary but can be anywhere from $0.13 to $0.24 per foot to develop and another $0.12 to $0.24 per foot to do the video transfer. This ranges from $9 to $17 per minute for all lab costs, *in addition to* the cost of the film stock. So overall you are looking at anywhere from $16 to $30 per minute when you shoot on 16mm film. This usually comes to a few hundred dollars for a five-minute short.

## Why Such Variety Among Costs?

Black-and-white film is different from color film, and the lab processes are different. Either black-and-white film or color film can also be shot on negative (similar to the film you buy for a regular still photo camera) or reversal film (similar to slide film). The costs are significantly different for these two processes.

Most film schools start students on black-and-white reversal film, which is less expensive than shooting on color negative, and it is also a better teaching tool because reversal film stock is relatively unforgiving (just like slide film)—you get what you shoot, and the lab cannot make up for errors.

When you shoot on negative, just as when you process a roll of film at your local photo lab, the lab can make adjustments to brightness if something comes out too dark or too overlit. If it's color, the lab can also shift the colors to one shade or another. This is not so with reversal, and it forces students to expose correctly the first time, and it is very revealing of the errors you make and why you made them.

Color reversal is a particular kind of look that is being used more and more in today's music videos (or often they won't shoot on reversal but alter the footage digitally to look like they did!).

Black-and-white reversal comes in two flavors: 200 ASA Tri-X, which looks very similar to Tri-X black-and-white you buy for a still photo camera, which is a standard of photojournalism the world over: gritty, dramatic, grainy, and high-contrast. Or 100 (Kodak recently changed the stock from 50 to 100 ASA) ASA Plus-X, which is fine grained and very sharp—among the sharpest of all film stocks ever made.

The ASA number (sometimes referred to also as ISO) refers to the sensitivity of the film, just like regular still photo film stock. The higher the number, the more sensitive it is. This number is used in conjunction with a light meter to determine how much light is necessary for the scene.

The movie *Pi,* directed by Darren Aronofsky, which won the Dramatic Directing Award in 1998 at the Sundance Film Festival, was shot entirely on black-and-white reversal. It's a good film to look at to see the qualities and capabilities of this film stock.

Color negative is the most widely used and most expensive film stock. Almost every movie you see in a theater is shot on color negative. It offers rich, "realistic" colors, a wide range of exposure latitude, and greater flexibility with the lab work. Anyone who is seriously interested in learning more about different film stocks and how they perform should consider a subscription to *American Cinematographer* magazine. You can find it at better magazine stores or order a subscription online.

And while you may not have access to a filmmaking class, you can learn a tremendous amount about motion picture cinematography by taking a regular photography course and working with a manual camera, lenses, film, lights, light meters, developing, and printing. The rules are the same for photography as for cinematography. The only major difference is that you don't usually have control over shutter speed in cinematography. All the other variables, aperture, film sensitivity, depth of field, shadows, and focusing, are the same.

If your only costs in making a film were the film and processing itself and you had a cast who worked for free and equipment you were able to borrow or steal, then a feature film shot on color negative 16mm would cost approximately eight to ten thousand dollars in total film costs if you shot economically and didn't waste footage, never doing more than a couple of takes.

This is how Robert Rodriguez made his first feature film, *El Mariachi,* and is also how the 2004 film *Primer,* written and directed by

Shane Carruth, was made, which won the Grand Prize at the 2004 Sundance Film Festival.

It is important to note, however, that these costs refer to the filming alone. After the editing is done in the computer, it is only viewable on video. In order to have it prepared for regular film projection in a theater, it must go through several additional and very expensive lab processes that are beyond the scope of this book. The producers of movies such as *El Mariachi* and *Primer* spent tens of thousands of dollars to make it to the big screen after the few thousand they spent to finish it first on video. Robert Rodriguez's book *Rebel Without a Crew: Or How a 23-Year-Old Filmmaker with $7,000 Became a Hollywood Player* outlines his struggles.

In general, you should assume that if you shoot on 16mm, your film is going to remain on video. It's costly and difficult to prepare 16mm for distribution and projection in regular movie theaters because movie theaters only project in 35mm, so the 16mm has to be transferred via a "blowup" process, which compromises its image quality when made available for big-screen projection.

The good news is that most film festivals will still exhibit your film on the big screen using a video projection. Festivals are friendly to many projection formats, whereas movie theaters are not.

## Why Shoot on Film If Your Product Is Going to End Up on Video Anyway?

Because it will still look like it was shot on film and join the ranks of decades of movies shot in the same way. Being shot on film often makes people take your work more "seriously" because it looks more conventionally like a real movie. Sixteen-millimeter film looks excellent on a television screen and very often cannot be distinguished from 35mm.

The same exact film stocks used by major Hollywood 35mm productions are available to you for a small 16mm production. If you shoot on 16mm, edit in your computer, and transfer your finished film to DVD, it will look like dynamite—if, of course, your lighting was done well!

There are several reasons that footage shot on film looks so different from that shot on video. Soap operas, for instance, and the nightly TV news are shot on video. They look quite a bit different from most movies you rent on video, don't they? Film stock and video chips translate colors and light in different ways: One is real chemistry; the other is digital or analog data. Film cameras and video cameras also have different lens systems and usually operate at different frame rates. Film has a grain to it that video does not. And video has a pixelation that film does not. All these issues and more contribute to vast differences between how film and video look.

One option that will significantly reduce the costs of shooting on film is to shoot without crystal sync. Remember, this means you are using a camera that does not keep a perfectly steady and consistent frame rate. Such cameras are called MOS cameras (more on that to follow) and can be relatively inexpensive to buy. It requires a different approach, but the results can be very rewarding.

While a very basic sync-sound camera might cost ten thousand dollars or much more, a Canon Scoopic, for example, which is a very easy 16mm MOS camera to use, can often cost less than fifteen hundred dollars, sometimes much less.

There are other similar cameras. But MOS cameras are much louder, because they weren't intended to be used for simultaneous sound recording (since they don't run a strict speed necessary for recording dialogue). Believe it or not, *El Mariachi* was actually shot in this way. None of the dialogue for this movie was recorded at the same moment the camera was running! It was recorded immediately after the film take, so the actor had the way he read the line fresh in his mind. Then the dialogue was matched up later, and any moving lips that didn't sync nicely were simply hidden by a cutaway shot.

Also, an entire genre of classic cinema—the Spaghetti Westerns

An excellent book to read for detailed information on the various 16mm cameras available today, both MOS and crystal sync, is *The 16mm Camera Book* by Douglas Underdahl. It can be purchased at http://longvalleyequip.com and can be ordered from any bookstore. It is a dynamite book that very clearly distinguishes between the dozens of makes, models, and designs of motion picture cameras—information that is normally very confusing and overwhelming, but is crucial to any novice.

by Sergio Leone—was shot MOS! ("MOS" refers to a shot, a sequence, or a film that is shot without sound, which is added later. "MOS" stands for "*Mit* Out Sound" and derives from an old Hollywood story about a German director asking for a shot to be filmed "*mit* out sound" and the camera assistant complying with this request by writing "MOS" on the slate.)

All the dialogue and sound effects were added later, and the results are stunning. It requires much more work, but it can also help keep you in line with the realities of filmmaking, namely that movies are ultimately a visual art and must be told visually. Working with an MOS camera requires that you keep the visuals your top priority and often leads to beautiful projects. Film schools always start students on MOS cameras.

A motion picture camera is a very complex machine, and any number of things can go bad over the years. If possible, order from an established camera store that offers a refund. Stores that clean and service their cameras before they sell them, as well as offer a warranty, are best. Two such places are: http://visualproducts.com and http://www.whitehouseav.com.

If you're thinking seriously about buying your own 16mm camera, be careful about where you get it. A common place to turn is eBay, but this source is risky because you don't know if the cameras people are selling actually work until you get your first footage back.

Shooting on film is a bit mysterious and magical. You never know exactly what you are going to get. If it comes out well, you will sit in awe of the feeling you have when you first get your footage back. Then editing will be an extraordinary joy.

# Part IV

# Dialogue
# and
# Characterization

I am a bear of very little brain, and long words bother me.
—WINNIE-THE-POOH

Every line of dialogue should either reveal character,
advance the story, or get a laugh.
—AUGUSTUS THOMAS

## Lecture 11

# You Talk Too Much. Get Some Boundaries. And Who Are You, Really? I Mean *Really*?

> What a character is grows out of what
> he has been and done.
> —KENNETH THORPE ROWE

Tell nothing. Show everything.

We are defined by what we do and what we say. In life and in screenplays.

When your characters talk, have them reveal only what is necessary to further the story. How long should a scene be? As long is it needs to be—within reason. Shorter is always preferable. Try not to go over four pages.

Release information gradually. You know how tedious it is when you meet people at a party or gathering and they reveal too much information about themselves too fast? After ten minutes they've told you half their life story, none of which you asked about or cared to know.

It's boring enough in life. It's really a drag in a screenplay. Talky scenes bog down screenplays. If you want to write long, dialogue-heavy scenes, write plays. Of course, there will be exceptions. But don't worry about the exceptions at this stage of your screenwriting career.

*Before you break the rules, learn the rules.*

In life, most of us are protective about who we are, unless circumstances require that we offer up personal information. If we must, we only let a few details slip out and we're careful about certain areas. We reveal facts about ourselves gradually, usually starting with the positive information. The longer we know someone, the more we may choose to get into the less attractive details.

As we get more and more comfortable with someone, we become more trusting and open.

You should keep that in mind when you write your characters, especially your lead.

## There's Not Much to Say About Dialogue

Dialogue can be lifelike or artificial. Lifelike is how people really talk. Artificial is sanitized lifelikeish dialogue. Much of the dialogue on bad TV sitcoms is artificial. Everybody's funny (in real life everyone isn't). Parents tend to be buffoons while the fourteen-year-olds are smart and wise.

Write how people talk.

Two goofball slackers in their twenties will talk differently than two devout nuns in their fifties.

In real life a clever person will say clever things. A dull person will not. In real life a clever person will be consistently clever or witty as he goes through each day. In your screenplay, most of the time we see a clever person, he *should* be the clever, witty guy—if *that's* the character's dramatic purpose. If you're writing that character for comic relief or to be a buddy/confidant to your protagonist, his job is to say or do funny things. We don't necessarily need to see the dark, sad, or unhappy aspects of his life. Sitcoms are good examples of this.

When you watch the best sitcoms, certain characters are always funny. Virtually every line out of their mouths gets a laugh. That's because in the twenty-two minutes of their show their sole purpose is to appear and say lines that will be funny and maybe further the plot. Check out reruns of *Frasier* and count the laughs that Niles gets. Same with Jack or Karen on *Will & Grace*. If we spent 24/7 with these characters, odds are they wouldn't be saying these funny, clever lines every time they opened their mouths. Yet in the context of their sitcoms, their lines are all funny.

Characters should speak in what appears to be their natural everyday language, but they must avoid the repetition and digression of ordinary conversation. What they say must be carefully designed to move the story forward.

Characters in screenplays (and every form of fiction) tend to be drawn from real life. Your success as a screenwriter will depend on your powers of observation and on your ability to portray what you observe. Characters are also drawn from what you read and what you hear.

Astute, observant screenwriters note the peculiarities, eccentricities, and special qualities of the people around them. Sometimes they'll create a character accurately drawn from a single living model. More often they'll use combinations of personalities that have moved or intrigued them to create a totally original character.

Ironically, characters who are comprised of various aspects of real people are often the best. There are few figures in real life that can be transplanted bodily to a screenplay and yet remain believable and effective. There is no rule for this labor. One writer will work marvels with materials that others can only botch into chaos.

Books and teachers can say little other than to warn against excess and to advise you to rely on personal knowledge.

Your ultimate source of material is life.

From what you see of people in all manner of circumstances you will select those traits of character that seem significant to you and right for your story. With practice and through the development skill, you will make these creations of yours credible and real and make them come alive on the pages of your script.

## Tell Me What Somebody Wants and I'll Tell You What He'll Say

When you're new to writing dialogue, it's often hard to figure out where to begin in a scene, assuming you even know where the scene will take place.

That's why characters need to want something. If you're writing a short screenplay about a guy who wakes up in the middle of the night with a craving for something sweet, *that's* your starting point.

Let's call him Nick.

It's 1:15 A.M. Nick wakes up with an appetite for Ben and Jerry's Cherry Garcia ice cream. He knows he bought a pint the day before and that he only ate half of it. He goes to the fridge and opens the freezer door only to find out that the ice cream's gone. He goes into his roommate's bedroom and sees him watching TV, the Cherry Garcia container on his chest as he's finishing off the last spoonful.

You know what Nick will say. He will be angry and accusatory. He might scream at his roommate. They might get into an argument. We might find out that Nick always steals the roommate's food and that this was a revenge thing. Or we might learn that Nick's roommate is selfish and is always eating Nick's food.

We might learn all kinds of things about both Nick and his roommate. We'll learn whatever the screenwriter wants us to learn. The scene can end in various ways: The roommates can make up, they can get into a fistfight, Nick can threaten to move, or the roommate—because it's his apartment—can kick Nick out.

Point is, the simple fact that Nick wanted a specific late-night comfort food resulted in a dramatic, confrontational scene.

The story isn't over, because one thing is certain: Because Nick is

still hungry for the Cherry Garcia ice cream, whatever words were exchanged, Nick will be storming out of the apartment in search of it.
The story won't be resolved until he gets it or doesn't get it.

If he gets it, it's a happy ending.

If he doesn't get it, it's an unhappy ending.

If he doesn't get it but instead discovers another type of sweet or,
better yet, meets a girl, then it's a satisfying ending.

Your lead character should be unique, sympathetic, and continuously interesting. Dialogue is not a substitute for character or plot.
Don't introduce too many characters simultaneously, because it will
confuse the reader. Don't give the audience information it already
knows.

# Before Jack Was Jack:
## The Lesson of *Five Easy Pieces*

Why don't you write books people can read?
—NORA JOYCE, TO HER HUSBAND, JAMES

Despite what I say about structure and plot and getting your story moving fast, there are always exceptions.

My favorite exception and one of my all-time favorite movies is *Five Easy Pieces,* which starred Jack Nicholson before he was a major star. By the time *Five Easy Pieces* hit theaters in 1970, Jack had acted in a bunch of low-budget films. *Easy Rider* had put him on the map.

*Five Easy Pieces* is more like a foreign film. It was what today would be called an independent film.

If you were in my class, I'd screen the film and there would be a discussion. Here I'm going to give you an overview of the plot and ask you to rent the film. If you've already seen it, rent it again.

*Five Easy Pieces* is a moody character study of an alienated drifter named Bobby Dupea (Nicholson) working as an oil rigger in Southern California. For nearly the first thirty minutes of the film nothing much happens in the way of plot. We just learn stuff about Bobby. He comes off like a hot-tempered redneck. He lives with a good-hearted but dim-witted waitress, drinks beer, goes bowling, and cheats on his girlfriend. The more we watch him, the more we get the feeling that he's uncomfortable in his own skin.

He seems restless and confused.

Finally, an Event happens, but not necessarily an Instigating Event. Out of context this may seem odd, but while stuck in a traffic jam Bobby gets out of his car, climbs onto the back of a pickup truck, spots an upright piano, and starts to play a classical piece.

This serves as a catalyst that makes us realize that maybe, just maybe, Bobby isn't what we think he is.

The actual Instigating Event comes when Bobby pays an unexpected visit to his sister. We didn't know he had a sister. He visits her at a recording studio where we learn that she is a classical pianist. Since we've just learned a few scenes back that he plays classical piano, that she does also tweaks our curiosity.

We learn that they haven't seen each other in a while. She then reveals something that gets the story moving and catapults us into Act Two: Their father isn't well. She suggests that Bobby visit him.

Reluctantly, Bobby agrees.

From this point on _Five Easy Pieces_ becomes thoroughly plot driven. Bobby ventures back home, reluctantly bringing his girlfriend with him.

On the way they pick up two lesbian hitchhikers whose car has broken down on their way to Alaska. This section with these two women is brief but provides some much-needed comic relief, not to mention a classic Jack scene in a diner. However, when you watch the movie, take note: The hitchhikers are unnecessary to the furthering of the plot. I've had discussions in my classes where people have disagreed and found reasons to justify the section. For example: The women are going to Alaska. That's where Bobby is headed at the end of the film. Perhaps they implanted the idea in his head. If Bobby didn't pick up the two women, the famous diner scene (in which Bobby goes head-to-head with a waitress) might not have been as effective, if only he and his girlfriend were at the table.

The very entertaining diner scene also serves to further illustrate Bobby's hotheaded, almost redneck personality, which we'll soon learn is in contrast to his upbringing. Again, is the scene necessary to the plot? Probably not. We already know Bobby quite well by now. But it's an enjoyable side trip on the script's primary journey.

Okay. Possible. My belief is that even though the primary story line didn't *need* the lesbian hitchhikers, the screenwriter went off on a tangent that's very entertaining.

Bobby and his girlfriend arrive at Puget Sound. We find out that he grew up in a beautiful home and comes from a family of serious musicians.

We realize that he has rejected this life and chosen the blue-collar, ordinary life of an oil rigger who lives with a country music–loving waitress.

Why?

That becomes one of the questions we, as audience members, want answered. While at home, Bobby seduces and falls in love with his older brother's fiancée. Bobby had brought his girlfriend with him, but before going to the family home he dropped her off at a motel with instructions to sit tight until he contacted her.

We also get a chance to see Bobby play another piece. We see that he's good.

We find out that he's protective of his sister (who has also arrived at the family digs) when he realizes she's involved with her father's male nurse.

There's lots of conflict and drama.

There's even a scene where Bobby attempts to reconcile with his father, the victim of a stroke, who may or may not be able to hear what Bobby says. But *we* hear what he says and we get a brief look into his soul.

One day Bobby's girlfriend shows up unannounced, much to Bobby's chagrin.

Finally, the situation gets too uncomfortable and complicated for

Bobby. By now we know he doesn't like discomfort and complications in his life. So he and his girlfriend leave to head back to California.

On the way, they stop for gas. While she goes to get coffee Bobby (and I'm simplifying this) hitches a ride with a trucker headed for Alaska.

The last shot of the movie is of the truck driving off as the girlfriend (did I mention she's pregnant?) wonders where Bobby is and what the hell is going on.

Fade Out.

The reason I love this movie and show it to all my classes is because it breaks the rules.

- It takes a long time to get started.
- It has a hero who isn't especially likable (and remember, this was made before Jack was Jack and he didn't have a huge fan base).
- It spends nearly thirty minutes establishing his world and who he is, which is *way too long.*
- It goes off on an unnecessary but fun tangent with the hitch-hikers.
- It introduces major characters well into the second act.
- Although the ending is satisfying, it leaves the audience with several questions.

The lesson of *Five Easy Pieces* is that a compelling, complicated three-dimensional main character with shadings, contours, and internal conflicts will hold an audience's attention.

But only for so long.

There must be a story.

No matter how interesting it is to watch the young Jack deal with his character's demons and angst, without the powerful story that eventually comes, our interest would eventually diminish.

# Part V

# Screenwriting

**Writing:** The act or art of forming visible letters or characters
that serve as visible signs of ideas, words, or symbols.
–MERRIAM-WEBSTER ONLINE

## Lecture 12

# On to the Full-Length Screenplay

Writing only leads to more writing.

–COLETTE

The best writing is rewriting.

–E. B. WHITE

Most new screenwriters are anxious to get started. They get their idea worked out in their heads, or maybe they've put a few thoughts on paper, and they go straight to Final Draft, Script Magic, or whatever screenwriting program they're going to use.

This is a mistake.

Putting your thoughts down in even the most basic cause-and-effect outline helps. It's good to know where the first act ends before you've written the first page. And it's *really* good to know where the second act ends. And if you're lucky enough to actually have an idea of what your third act will be, you are on the road to nirvana.

I've found that some screenwriters, both new and experienced, are incapable of thinking things out ahead of time. They have no other choice than to "just start writing" and hope they'll find their way. But most of the screenwriters I've worked with get to be very good at plotting out their scripts due to the simple fact that I force them to do it. While I can't force you, I can tell you that you should.

Some struggle through the process. Others find that it's not as painful as they thought, and most find it to be lifesaving.

I try to make those who reject it understand that sooner or later they will run into a brick wall. By doing even the roughest outline of their idea they might avoid plot obstacles later on.

## The Third Act Blues

Most people have trouble getting into Act Three and figuring out how their story will end. I believe that if you can get to the end of Act Two you're in a good place. Certainly a better place than the person who has done little, if any, prethinking and starts the writing process by facing an empty page 1 with no particular place to go.

Although I personally have trouble with third acts in my outlines, I consider it a moral victory to get to the end of Act Two, see what I have, then start writing the script.

## Different Kinds of Outlines

I'm a big believer in outlines. What an outline does is give you a blueprint or road map of where your story is heading. You won't have any dialogue in an outline. Just narrative.

It's pretty much cause and effect. Some people in the industry call this a Beat Sheet. You basically list fifteen to twenty (or more) key plot points with bullets:

- This happens
- This happens
- This happens
- Then it spins off this way
- Then that way
- Then it takes a turn here
- Then we find out this

- Then it goes that way
- And so on ... until you get to a resolution

A Beat Sheet is better than nothing, but in my opinion it's not nearly thorough enough.

A better approach, but not necessarily the best, is a general outline in narrative. You basically summarize what's going to happen in greater detail than the Beat Sheet, but you don't specify act breaks or use dialogue.

## SHORT OUTLINE SAMPLE

### GROWL

**BASIC PREMISE**

Five high school students in upstate New York making a low-budget horror movie about Bigfoot are captured by a <u>real</u> tribe living in the Catskill Mountains. But the tribe is <u>entirely female</u>. Every 10 years they need to increase the population. Since there are no male Bigfeet, they kidnap young men hiking or camping in the woods and use them to breed with young Bigfoot females. Then they kill the men. The kids (four guys, one girl) must find a way to escape, but before they do some die and one falls in love with a female Bigfoot.

**STORY LINE**

Five high school seniors with a camera, money from one of their uncles and a dream to make a movie that will be their calling card to Hollywood decide to make a low-budget horror movie about Bigfoot.

Each of the kids has a different stake in the project: one as director, one as screenwriter, one as producer and two as lead actors. They all, however, will act in the film.

Because they live in upstate New York, they decide that the Catskill Mountains will be a perfect substitute for the lush forests of Washington State where most Bigfoot sightings occur.

They plan to shoot the movie over a long weekend.

We open by introducing the kids and establishing the power structure. The nerdy smart kid wrote the script. The big-mouth/smart-ass is directing. The shrewd, obnoxious kid with the rich uncle is producing, the airhead/anorexic girl is the female lead and the vain, arrogant star of their high school plays is the male lead.

With one car and a minivan they head up to the mountains to shoot. Along the way, in an argument between the screenwriter and director about the accuracy of the script, we learn key information about Bigfoot. The nerdy writer believes with his heart and soul that Bigfoot is real. Everyone else thinks it's bullshit.

They arrive at the first set. Start shooting. After a few scenes are shot, while setting up for another, one of the guys is grabbed by "something" and carried away. The others look for him. Can't find him. Then another is grabbed. Then another.

Then all of them. The last one grabbed is the nerdy writer. He stares into the face of a Bigfoot.

Rather than be scared out of his wits, he's elated. He's been proven right. They do exist.

The five kids find themselves held prisoner in a cell, being watched by two stern-looking Bigfeet who seem to be talking. The nerdy writer observes that they are female. As other Bigfeet of varying ages stare at the kids, the writer notices that they all are female.

Each of the kids is reacting according to his or her personality. The actress is scared out of her mind. The actor is whining like a baby. The director is figuring out how to incorporate this into the script. The producer wants to junk the movie and make a documentary. The nerdy writer is in a state of wonder.

Later. Night. The kids are huddled together, sleeping. Then they hear a voice from outside the cell. It's a human. A gorgeous blonde. Seventeen. She fills them in on the lay of the land.

Turns out that there is a small but thriving Bigfoot community living in caves and underground. As for her, she was found abandoned by humans in the woods. The Bigfeet

saved her life and raised her as one of
them. She informs the kids that Bigfeet are
able to speak if necessary but that they
usually communicate in a sign language. The
younger ones prefer to speak. This is when
she reveals that there are only female
Bigfeet. She explains that male Bigfeet were
wiped out decades ago by a pesticide in the
forest that somehow only affected males.

She explains that every decade the tribe
replenishes itself. They accomplish this by
capturing men who are hiking or camping in
the woods.

The next news jolts everyone: If a man is
unable to impregnate a Bigfoot female, he is
killed. The blonde explains that most men
fail due to either the inability to achieve
an erection or a low sperm count.

Then she tells them the really bad news:
The guy who successfully impregnates one female must service them all. Because the
creatures are so hairy and ugly, this would
be a fate worse than death.

Hearing this, the kids, especially the
guys, realize they have to escape. The blonde
says it's impossible. People have tried.
These kids are going to give it a shot.

But before they do, one by one the guys
are readied for sex. This entails being
given certain foods to enhance their diets,
mainly herbs and berries.

Meanwhile, one of the guys (the director)
falls hard for the blonde. Because she's hu-

man he wants to help her get back to civilization, but to his surprise, she doesn't want to leave. She's afraid to go back.

The airhead actress isn't in danger. In fact, she makes friends with the blonde and young female Bigfeet, giving them makeup and fashion tips.

The nerdy screenwriter—who can't get a girl at school—falls head over heels in love with a teenage female Bigfoot.

One by one, the guys are eliminated, primarily for not being up to snuff in the sack.

The one who succeeds is the director, but only because of the promise of having sex with the blonde. Also, by this point the nerd is in love with his Bigfoot girlfriend.

<u>The Twist</u> at the end is that the blonde isn't human at all but an aberration in the species, whose only purpose was to turn on the director. She lied about the pesticide wiping out the male Bigfeet. Truth is, the Bigfoot world is a matriarchal society. Men are only used for procreation and discarded. Even the males that are conceived are destroyed.

The film ends with only the nerdy writer surviving and returning to civilization with the young female Bigfoot. He points out that with a little plastic surgery and lots of electrolysis she'll get along fine.

The End

Registered WGA, East by D. B. Gilles

It's always wise to register everything you write with the Writers Guild of America: screenplays, treatments, and outlines. You can do it online. Depending upon which part of the country you reside in, go to www.wgaeast.org or www.wgawest.org and follow the registration instructions.

Although the general outline lays out the plot and includes a few twists and turns, it's still not very detailed, especially when it comes to act breaks.

In my screenwriting classes I encourage my students to do a three-act story line that can be anywhere from five to seven pages long.

Here's an example:

### THREE-ACT STORY LINE SAMPLE

MIDNIGHT SNACK

**BASIC PREMISE**

Modest, low-key chef loses his job at an exclusive restaurant because of his lack of personal flamboyance and his unimaginative recipes. To save his career he decides to reinvent himself as a flashy, 300-pound, bigger-than-life chef from the Southwest with colorful, fattening regional dishes.

He becomes a superstar chef, bestselling author and host of his own show on the Food Network. But his newfound success and wealth become unsatisfying because he's not being true to himself and he's fallen for a woman who's in love with his reinvented self.

## ACT ONE

Open by introducing RANDY DUFORE, the chef of a struggling Los Angeles restaurant specializing in French peasant cooking. Business is slipping and the owner fires Randy for the simple reason that it's the era of the celebrity chef like Emeril Lagasse, Paul Prudhomme, Wolfgang Puck, with flamboyant personalities and colorful takes on different cuisines.

Randy is devastated. His credentials are impeccable. He studied at two of the best cooking schools in Europe and apprenticed at three major American restaurants.

The one thing he lacks is charisma. That can't be taught.

He licks his wounds by going back to his hometown in Oklahoma. He spends time with the person who got him interested in cooking in the first place: his grandmother, who raised him. She still runs the small restaurant where Randy cut his teeth. We learn that despite Randy's fine education in Continental cuisine, his roots are in down-home Southwestern food. We also find out that he was more than a little ashamed of where he came from.

Randy and his grandmother have a soul-searching talk in which she says that every chef has to find his niche. If one cuisine doesn't click, find another. If that doesn't work, keep looking to find what works, then stay with it.

Before returning to Los Angeles, Randy has lunch at a small roadhouse diner where he observes a wisecracking, overweight Mexican short-order cook with a huge handlebar mustache regaling his customers as he serves up fattening, delectable Southwestern/Tex-Mex dishes.

Inspiration strikes. Randy models himself after the Mexican cook, goes back to LA, hires an acting coach, resurrects the Southern accent he spent years trying to lose, dons a wig, grows a handlebar mustache and, through padding, makes himself appear to weigh 300 pounds.

He then presents himself as TUCKER LEE PETTIBONE.

Using the many down-home recipes he learned from his grandmother as a boy, he sets out to start a new career.

ACT TWO

After a few minor setbacks, largely due to his inability to stay in the "Tucker Lee" character, he gets a job. The restaurant is a success, and so is "Tucker." While Randy would stay in the kitchen at the restaurant he was fired from, "Tucker" works the room. Everybody loves him.

In short order, things take off. His flamboyance gets him a deal for a cookbook, then his own cooking show on the Food Network.

Things go great for him, except for two things: First, he falls in love with a woman

who digs fat guys, so he has to pretend he's
this hugely overweight guy all the time.
This presents problems when it comes to sex.
A subplot deals with the woman trying to get
him in bed and him constantly finding ways to
avoid getting naked in front of her and thus
exposing that he really isn't who he says he
is.

In one scene, without his "fat" disguise,
Randy attempts to make conversation with the
woman, but because he's thin and low-key
she's not interested. So Randy knows that to
be with her he has to play Tucker Lee Pettibone to the hilt.

Second, as fame and fortune come, his ego
gets the better of him and he wants the
world to know who he really is.

But he's afraid that the "real" person
won't be as accepted as his flamboyant alter
ego and he's even more concerned that the
girl won't be interested in his "thin and
trim" self.

So he's forced to live life as a big, fat
fraud.

To further complicate the situation, a
snobbish female Food Critic begins to suspect that Tucker Lee Pettibone isn't for
real. Because Randy has fabricated an entire
backstory for "Tucker," when the Food Critic
tries to verify some of the biographical
data she comes up blank. She then sets out
to find out just who Tucker Lee Pettibone really is.

The critic ultimately discovers the truth and confronts Randy. She decides to blackmail him. She'll keep his secret for a piece of the action in his new restaurant, as well as a percentage of his book royalties.

If he doesn't agree, she'll go public and expose him.


ACT THREE

Randy has reached a turning point. He's so frustrated from pretending to be Tucker Lee that he's almost relieved the jig is up. But what's tearing him apart is the fact that the woman he's crazy about (who is turned on by fat guys) won't be interested in him when she finds out that he's really thin—and that he lied.

He decides to come clean with the truth during a live broadcast of his cooking show on the Food Network.

He does so.

And he reverts back to his modest, low-key self.

To his surprise, he's accepted by his fans. Turns out that the arrogant, egomaniacal chef prototype is fading fast and the more humble, down-to-earth type is far more desirable. More important, Randy accepts the fact that while he may have disguised who he was, <u>the recipes are his</u>. We'll have seen that he combined his European training with his grandmother's recipes to create sensational food.

As far as the girl who likes fat guys

goes, she drops him, but Randy and the producer of his cooking show (who has always
had a crush on him) get together.

Theme of the story: Sometimes you have to
become someone else to find out who you are.

The End

Registered WGA, East by D. B. Gilles

The most intricate and difficult form of outlining is the treatment. Treatments are much longer and more detailed than the previous examples. I've seen and written treatments upward of thirty pages. By definition, a treatment is an original story written for motion picture purposes in a form suitable for use as the basis of a screenplay.

A treatment is essentially a scene-by-scene breakdown of the screenplay with dialogue that forces you to think out your entire movie in great detail.

Writing one is a challenge. I believe all screenwriters should know how to write a treatment so they are prepared for when they *have* to write one. A producer may like a script you've already written. He may ask you if you have any other ideas. You'll tell him a couple that you've been thinking about, and he may like one. He might tell you to give him a treatment. Or he may come to you with an idea of his and ask you to write a treatment. He may even *pay* you for this.

If you don't know how to write one, you're screwed.

There are two reasons to learn how to write a treatment: in anticipation of the day when you are asked to write one and because certain ideas you have might be too intimidating to tackle as screenplays. By doing the treatment first you will be able to think it through and possibly work through some of the problems before you write it as a screenplay.

What follows is an example of a treatment. You'll see act breaks, dialogue, a story that moves along at a good pace, and a satisfying ending.

## TREATMENT SAMPLE

MORBID FASCINATION

**BASIC PREMISE**

A Funeral Home in a northern Pennsylvania town is bought by a national chain. As soon as the new owners take over, business starts booming, but most of the people dying aren't old—<u>they're high school and college students</u>. When the 17-year-old boy who works part-time at the Home stumbles onto the new owner's diabolical plan, he and his girlfriend must fight to the death to prevent their own.

(Yes. I know. Another funeral home story.)

ACT ONE

A dozen high school cheerleaders in shorts and T-shirts are practicing a new routine. A black Lexus with tinted windows is parked nearby. The driver watches the girls. He doesn't stare at them lustfully. It's more of a calculated look. There's something odd about his left hand—the tip of his index finger is missing.

Driver gets out of the Lexus, goes to a new Volkswagen Beetle. Checks if anyone's looking. Crouches down. Attaches something to a tire. Goes back to the Lexus.

Practice ends. The girls disperse. Three

of them—a blonde and two brunettes—get in the Volkswagen. Take off. We hear some girl talk, how one's getting screwed over by a guy. The others advise her on what to do.

Lexus follows the VW onto the freeway. Driver smokes a corncob pipe. He waits for the right moment; then, when the VW tries to pass a Mack truck, Lexus driver lifts a remote control from his pocket. Presses a button. VW's tire blows. VW swerves into the Mack truck.

CUT TO—The face of the blond cheerleader. Looks like she's sleeping. But she's not. She's dead. And she's lying naked on a table in the embalming room of a Funeral Home. On separate tables are the two other cheerleaders. Two male morticians are preparing the girls for viewing.

DISSOLVE TO—The girls being dressed, made up, placed in coffins, then wheeled into separate viewing rooms.

Later. Mourners fill the viewing room where the blonde is laid out. Her mother can't stop crying. A hand holding a box of tissues comes into frame. The dead girl's mother nods gratefully, then takes a few tissues.

On closer inspection of the hand offering the tissue box, we see that the tip of the index finger is *missing*.

CAMERA PULLS OUT of the room. Outside, giving full view of the Funeral Home, coming to rest on a sign:

### DEVONSHIRE MORTUARIES
Serving the people of
Tremont, Arizona

DISSOLVE TO—ANOTHER SIGN, 2,000 MILES AWAY

### SHELLERTON FUNERAL HOME
Victor Shellerton
Funeral Director
Established 1906
Overton, Pennsylvania

SUPER: 6 MONTHS LATER

PAN UP to reveal a creepy old building. Spooky and foreboding, like a haunted house from a '50s horror film.

Inside. The place is neat but run-down. Of the four large viewing rooms <u>none</u> has a body in it. In the embalming room, HAZEL, the Home's cosmetologist, is doing the hair on an elderly female corpse.

The owner, 68-year-old VICTOR SHELLERTON— unsmiling, dour, tough—is in his office meeting with two representatives of Devonshire Mortuaries, the conglomerate that wants to buy his Funeral Home. With him are his wife and two assistants.

DAVIS CRAWLEY, 40, is the spokesman for Devonshire Mortuaries. He looks nothing like a Funeral Director. Handsome, trim, charming, wearing J Crew. You'd think he was a Yuppie ad executive or TV weatherman.

Davis is giving Mr. Shellerton reasons why he should sell the Funeral Home. "Just like the mom-and-pop grocery store is a thing of the past," says Davis, "so is the family-run Funeral Home. You're out of touch with modern funeral service practices. You're not maximizing your profit potential." Davis also points out that they bought the town's other Funeral Home, which they're shutting down, and that the owners were quite pleased with the price.

Victor's wife chimes in, "We've barely eked out a living for years. If we sell, maybe we can enjoy our retirement years." Even Victor's assistants say selling's a good idea. But no matter what anyone says, Victor doesn't want to sell.

In the hallway outside the office, someone is listening.

It's CLANCY BRUCK, 17. He works part-time at the Funeral Home, doing odd jobs and yard work. He's a senior in high school and plans on being a Funeral Director. Because of where he works and what he wants to be, combined with the fact that he's tall and gawky and resembles Ichabod Crane, Clancy takes his share of crap.

His high school paper voted him Student Most Likely to Rob a Grave.

MEANWHILE—Victor orders Davis and his associate to leave. Clancy watches Davis exit the Funeral Home and get into his car. Peer-

ing from a window, Clancy makes eye contact
with Davis. Davis nods at him. Smiles. Clancy
smiles back.

It's as if some primal connection has be-
gun.

Davis's car pulls out onto the street and
is almost cut off by a skinhead punk in a
souped-up Mustang. Davis angrily honks the
horn. The kid gives Davis the finger, peels
away.

Davis writes down the Mustang's license
plate number.

From the rear entrance ZACK MORAN, 50s,
comes in. He's the embalmer of the home.
Crusty and cool, but a drinker. Clancy likes
Zack. Clancy fills in Zack on the fact that
Devonshire Mortuaries wants to buy the fu-
neral home.

For the first time we see how Clancy feels
about it. He thinks the place should be
sold. It is old-fashioned, just like Davis
said. Zack has a different view. Big Funeral
Home chains have no soul. They come into a
community and make death and bereavement
more like shopping at The Gap or Starbucks.
"It's all about personal touch, Clancy. You
don't get that with conglomerates." Clancy
considers the remark.

Clancy at home. He lives in a modest house
with his mother, BETH, late 30s. His father
died when he was nine. Clancy's room suggests a kid with a morbid fascination with
death. Many books on burial customs, death

and dying, cemeteries around the world where celebrities are buried, magazines on the funeral industry. Several photographs of Clancy and his dad are on Clancy's nightstand.

That night. Behind Shellerton's Funeral Home. There are two garages; one houses the hearses and limousines, the other the personal cars of Victor and his wife. <u>Someone</u> is inside, doing <u>something</u> to the brakes of Victor Shellerton's Honda Accord. It's the guy with the missing fingertip

Next morning. A viewing room. Victor and one of his assistants wheel the coffin containing the elderly woman we saw earlier in the embalming room. He adjusts the coloring of her face with some mortician makeup. Fluffs her hair.

Victor's Pinto pulls out of the Home's parking lot. The black Lexus we saw before follows him. The driver is lighting his corncob pipe. We see the index finger with the missing tip. Victor turns onto a winding road. He applies the brakes. At first, no problem, but he senses that something's wrong. Then the Lexus makes its move, pulling alongside, then in front of Victor. He slams on the brakes. They don't work. Swerves. Crashes into a huge oak. Dead.

Clancy at school. He's not the most popular guy. Most kids ignore him; some snicker; a few toss out jibes, calling him names like Bela La<u>Grossy</u>, Count Suckula or Cemetery Boy. One of the guys giving him shit is the skinhead who drove the Mustang that cut Davis off. "Ever get laid in a coffin?" he sneers. "Probably the only chick you'd have a shot with is a dead one. And even then it's doubtful." Skinhead and his buddies laugh.

Clancy has two friends: TISH DOWLING, 17, is the daughter of the Head Groundskeeper of the county cemetery. She's taken a lot of crap about that. She lives in a house across the street from the cemetery. Tish is also Clancy's girlfriend and an Internet geek. OZZIE DEVANE, 17, is the son of the town's only openly lesbian woman. She runs a gas station. He's embarrassed that his mom is a lesbian but proud that she's the best car mechanic in town.

Clancy's house. His mother's about to go on a date with WALT JEFFRIES, Chief of Police in the small town they live in. Clancy doesn't like Walt. Clancy is very protective of her and thinks she could do better.

Shellerton's Funeral Home. Inside. Victor's body is in the embalming room, being worked on by Zack.

A cemetery. Victor's coffin rests atop the grave site in the family plot. A large crowd listens to a minister say a prayer. Clancy is there with Tish, his mother, Beth, and Walt, who's in his police uniform. Clancy looks up and in the distance, leaning against a mausoleum, is Davis Crawley, dressed in black.

Once again, they nod at each other. Tish notices this.

The wreckage of Victor's car. Walt Jeffries and JO, Ozzie's mother (the lesbian mechanic), are examining it. Jo remarks that it looks as if the brake linings might've been tampered with, but she can't be 100% sure because the force of the crash crushed everything.

Next day. Mrs. Shellerton is signing the papers to sell the Home to Devonshire Mortuaries. She hands the signed document to Davis. They shake hands.

Later. Clancy shows up for work. He sees Zack and the two Assistant Funeral Directors, as well as Hazel, the cosmetologist, packing up their personal stuff. Zack explains that they've all been fired. Clancy is upset for them and concerned for himself. We learn here that Victor Shellerton had agreed to give Clancy an apprenticeship in four years, after he finishes college, where he'll be majoring in Mortuary Management.

Zack tells Clancy to talk to Davis. Nervously, Clancy does so. They learn they have a lot in common. Like Clancy, Davis was raised by his mother. "Are you close to your mom?" asks Davis. Clancy nods yes. "A boy should be close to his mother," says Davis. "I'm where I am today because of her. She sacrificed everything for me. Show your mom love and respect. Do what she tells you. A mother will never lead you down the wrong path."

Davis asks Clancy why he wants to be a Funeral Director. He explains that his father died in a construction accident. The body was disfigured. There was a closed coffin service. Clancy never got to see his father one last time. He wants to be in a position to help reconstruct damaged bodies so other people won't experience his loss.

The meeting goes well. Davis permits Clancy to keep his part-time job and agrees to sponsor his apprenticeship when he finishes college. Davis then says that they'll be doing some renovation over the next few weeks but that Clancy can continue to show up. "We'll find something for you to do."

Clancy leaves with a handshake. He's on cloud nine.

He goes out to the yard to do some work. Unbeknownst to him, Davis watches him from a window. Suddenly, appearing next to him is an elderly gray-haired WOMAN. Davis points at Clancy. The elderly woman nods and smiles.

Night. A cemetery. Clancy, Tish and Ozzie make their way amidst the monuments and mausoleums. We see the dates on some. They're a hundred years old. This is the oldest section of the cemetery. They make their way to one particular mausoleum, then sneak inside.

INSIDE THE MAUSOLEUM—It's more like a

clubhouse. Long-dead bodies have disinte-
grated. This is where these three outcasts
hang. Ozzie has beer. He's bummed out because he doesn't get along with his mother's
new girlfriend. Clancy whines about his
mother dating Walt the cop. Tish chimes in
that at least their parents are trying to
find romance: "My parents haven't had sex in
five years." Clancy is also conflicted about
Victor Shellerton's death. He feels sad that
the old guy died and that everyone lost
their jobs, but he's pumped about working
for Davis. Tish gets on his case. We learn
she's not happy that he wants to be a Funeral Director in light of her father's profession as grave digger.

SERIES OF SHOTS of work being done on the
Home. Instead of its depressing color, it's
painted white with yellow trim. Inside, spacious viewing rooms are being redesigned
into efficient, smaller viewing areas. Outside, the parking lot is being enlarged.

The upstairs living quarters—quite large,
several bedrooms—are also being renovated
to accommodate a staff. Furniture is brought
in. A new wing is added downstairs to serve
as a postburial reception hall. Yet another
structure is built on the property: a crematorium. New hearses and limos arrive.
Brochures and pamphlets on the various
forms of burial and funeral arrangements
are made. Small advertisements are placed

on restaurant place mats, in church bul-
letins. Billboards go up around town. A local bowling team sports T-shirts sponsored
by Devonshire Mortuaries.

Clancy is trimming hedges. Davis calls him
inside and introduces him to four Assistant
Funeral Directors—three males and one female
in their mid-20s. Again, they look more like
Yuppie bankers than morticians. Let's call
them TOM, DICK, HARRY and MARY. Mary's gorgeous and radiates sexuality.

Davis tells Clancy there's someone else
he'd like him to meet. They go upstairs to
the living quarters. Someone is playing the
piano. Davis calls out, "Mom?" Sitting at
the piano is GRACE CRAWLEY, late 60s, pleasant, soft-spoken. The elderly woman we saw
in the window before. "This is the boy I was
telling you about, Mom," says Davis. Grace
and Clancy exchange pleasantries; then Davis
and Clancy go downstairs.

"She's going to be staying with me for a
while," says Davis.

CUT TO—THE FINISHED PRODUCT. What was once
a big, ugly, depressing monstrosity now
looks like a cheerful, spacious country bed-
and-breakfast.

The Shellerton Funeral Home sign outside
the Home. Suddenly, it's yanked out of the
ground. A beat, then a new sign replaces it:

## DEVONSHIRE MORTUARIES
### Davis Crawley
### Funeral Director
### Serving the people
### of Overton, Pennsylvania

Clancy and Tish pull up and park across the street. They look at the renovated Funeral Home. Clancy beams with pride. "Now <u>that's</u> what a Funeral Home should look like."

Says Tish, "Looks more like an International House of Pancakes. All they need is a grand-opening sign and an Early Bird Special."

Later. Inside the mausoleum at the cemetery. Clancy and Tish have just finished having sex. They cuddle. "This screwing in cemeteries makes me long for the days when kids had sex in the backseat," Tish says.

Next day. Clancy at work. He encounters Davis and remarks on how great the place looks. Davis agrees.

"Now all we need are some bodies," says Clancy.

"They'll come," says Davis.

Clancy's unsure, saying that barely one body a week came in during the time he worked for Mr. Shellerton. Sometimes there were two bodies. Clancy then adds that there aren't a lot of old people in town. They retire and move away.

"The bodies will come, son," says Davis ominously.

For the first time, Clancy gets an odd vibe from Davis.

CUT TO—The skinhead in the Mustang who cut Davis off and hassled Clancy. Shirtless and in cutoffs, he's working on his car in his driveway. The black Lexus stops across the street. From inside the driver watches the kid. The kid sees the car. Stares at it. Comes toward it. Pounds on the window, blurting, "What the hell you lookin' at?"

The tinted window lowers. Skinhead notices the missing index finger on driver's left hand. Driver asks directions. Skinhead points; driver thanks him. As skinhead goes back to his car, driver raises a gun—not a regular gun but a dart gun. Fires. The dart hits skinhead in the back of the neck. He reacts. Thinks it's a bee sting. Rubs it. Tries to shake it off.

Lexus takes off. Driver lights his corncob pipe.

Later. Skinhead eats supper with his family. He suddenly can't breathe. Holds his head. Screams. Convulses. Dies.

Davis in his office. Phone rings. "Devonshire Mortuaries, Davis Crawley speaking." A beat. "You have my deepest sympathy. I suggest you come over right now."

Davis makes funeral arrangements with the skinhead's grief-stricken parents. He tallies up the bill. Five thousand, four hundred dollars. "We take cash, check and, of course, we accept Visa, Mastercard and Diners Club."

Skinhead is on a slab in the embalming room. Davis and his Assistant Funeral Directors stand over the freshly embalmed body.

"It begins," says Assistant Tom.

"That it does," says Davis as he looks at the dead teen and smirks.


ACT TWO

Next day. Clancy at work. He peeks into the viewing room where the skinhead is laid out. Kid looks like an altar boy now. Shaved. In a suit and tie. Clancy looks at him and remarks, "To answer your question, I never did have sex in a coffin, but I get laid in a mausoleum twice a week. Asshole."

Cemetery. Skinhead's funeral. Family and friends watch as coffin is lowered into ground. TIME CUT: Davis stands over grave as grave diggers are shoveling the last pile of dirt.

A keg party is in progress at the local college. Deafening music. A hundred drunken college kids are carousing in a frat house. Parked outside is the black Lexus.

From inside the driver is using a telescope to study the drunk students. His corncob pipe rests in the ashtray. He's concentrating on the cars leaving the party. Watches until he spots one crammed with eight students—four guys, four girls.

When that car takes off, the Lexus follows.

Inside the car. Music blares, more drinking's going on, one kid's puking, a guy and girl are making out and the rest are laughing and being stupid. The car comes to a narrow country bridge; then the Lexus makes its move, forcing the kids' car through the railing and into the river below.

The Lexus stops. Driver gets out. Walks to the railing and looks down as the car sinks quickly into the dark water.

CUT TO—The car has been hauled out of the river and the bodies of the drowned college kids are on the riverbank covered with sheets.

Inside Devonshire Mortuaries. Davis and his four assistants are each counseling bereaved parents there to make funeral arrangements. Davis and his people are cool and smooth, behaving with great compassion and even greater salesmanship, pushing hard for the costliest services.

The bodies of seven of the eight drowned students lie in the embalming room at Devonshire Mortuaries. Davis is talking with Assistants Harry and Dick, who are dressed in work clothes as they prepare to work on the bodies.

"We got seven out of eight," says Davis. "One kid was visiting from out of state, so a mortuary in his hometown claimed him."

"How much did we make?" asks Assistant Dick.

"Highest was nine thousand; lowest was

forty-one hundred. Grand total: thirty-two thousand, seven hundred and fifty bucks."

Assistant Dick nods, then proceeds to the body of one of the dead girls. He removes the sheet. Checks out her breasts. Touches one. Mutters to himself, "What a waste."

CUT TO—NEWSPAPER HEADLINE:

**8 Shellerton University Students Drown Each, Including Driver, Legally Drunk**

Clancy's mom, Beth, is reading the paper at the breakfast table. Clancy enters. Sees headline. He's shocked. His mom asks if he knew any of the college students who died. He says he knew of two. We learn here that the area is considered suburban/country. Lots of baby boomers settled here in the 80s to raise their families. Now their kids flood three area high schools and the college.

Phone rings. It's Davis calling for Clancy. He asks if Clancy can come to work that night and the next to help with the parking. Because the seven student bodies have filled up the mortuary, Davis expects a madhouse. Clancy asks his mom. She says okay as long as he gets his homework done. Clancy tells Davis it's cool. Davis tells him to bring a friend to help. There'll be fifty bucks in it for him. Clancy calls Ozzie.

Parking lot. Sure enough, dozens of cars, filled with mourners, mainly college students. Clancy and Ozzie are directing traffic. As things die down, they take a break. Ozzie smokes a joint. Out of nowhere, Mary, the sexy Assistant Funeral Director, appears. Clancy introduces her to Ozzie. He cracks a couple of jokes. She laughs. From the look in her eyes, Ozzie might get lucky tonight.

Later. After the last car has pulled out, Davis hands Clancy and Ozzie $50 each. The boys thank Davis. Ozzie tells Clancy that he's going to stick around and get to know Mary better. Clancy then goes to his car to leave. But it doesn't start. Battery's dead. Davis offers to drive him home.

Embalming room. Assistant Mary is giving Ozzie a tour of the "workroom," as she calls it. Explaining the function of the bizarre-looking tools of the mortician. Ozzie only half-listens because he's so taken with Mary's gorgeousness—but the audience will be receiving important information for later.

Clancy's house. He invites Davis in to meet his mom. We sense that Clancy would like his mom and Davis to hit it off.

Davis turns on the charm. Unlike Walt, who has no social skills, Davis is flirtatious, flattering, and knows exactly what to say to a woman. Beth blushes. She's clearly taken with him. She invites him in for coffee. Clancy leaves them alone, purportedly to study.

A few hours later. As Davis leaves he asks Beth out for dinner. She accepts.

Embalming room. Assistant Mary and Ozzie are naked and screwing on an embalming table. To add a little shock value, while they're doing it the table rolls into another embalming table. Ozzie notices a body on it. He asks Mary if there's someplace else they can go. She says sure.

CUT TO—The coffin selection room. Filled with two dozen coffins of varying styles and prices. In one of them we find Ozzie and Mary screwing.

Next day at school. Ozzie tells Clancy about sleeping with Mary. Ozzie then shocks him by saying that he thinks he wants to be a Funeral Director.

Davis and Beth on their date. Dinner at a nice restaurant. They talk mostly about Clancy. We find out that he developed his morbid fascination with death after his father died. Beth isn't sure where Clancy got the idea of becoming a Funeral Director. She thinks it might be a phase. "Being a mortician isn't a bad way to make a living," Davis says. "It's a way of helping people. That's how I look at it."

In front of Clancy's house. Davis walks Beth to the door. They kiss. Clancy watches from his room. It's an innocent kiss. He feels good about it.

Somebody else is watching, too. Walt the cop. In his patrol car. When Davis pulls away, Walt follows him. Davis stops in front of one of the local high schools. Notices a sign announcing a big football game on Friday night. Marks it down. On the road, Davis guns it and runs a changing red light. Walt pulls him over. Gives him a reprimand and a ticket. Davis is pissed. He checks out Walt's full name. After he gets the ticket Davis writes down "Walt Jeffries" on a piece of paper.

High school football game in progress. Grandstands filled to capacity with cheering students and fans. Even Clancy, Tish and Ozzie are there. With Ozzie is Mary.

Parking lot. Amidst the school busses that transport the players, band and cheerleaders is the black Lexus. The driver is attaching something to the gas tank of one of the busses. It's a timer. It begins ticking.

Football game is over.

Twenty or so members of the high school marching band load into the bus with the timer on the gas tank, dressed in their nerdy uniforms. Bus takes off. Inside, the kids are laughing, horsing around.

The Lexus isn't far behind. As the bus heads out of the parking lot and onto a main road, the Lexus driver picks up something from the seat that looks like a remote control. He waits until the bus stops in front of an open field away from other cars and buildings, then presses a button.

Under the bus a small leak in the gas tank starts. As the bus drives along, sparks from the road ignite both the gasoline trail and the gas tank.

The bus explodes.

CUT TO—Embalming room of Devonshire Mortuaries. Bodies (20) of the dead band members are on the slabs waiting to be worked on; others are piled in corners. Davis and his assistants work feverishly. They're overwhelmed.

Zack's house. Zack's the embalmer who was fired early on by Davis. He's drinking. Phone rings. It's Davis. He explains that they need additional help and asks Zack if he'd like to make some fast cash. Zack agrees.

Zack works side by side with Assistants Tom, Dick, Harry and Mary. Mary catches his eye. He remarks that in his day there weren't many women in the business. Then he says that business sure has picked up since Devonshire took over. Dick overhears what Zack said, looks at him suspiciously.

Davis in his office, doing the books. Punches in the figure $110,000. He's talking to someone in the room. It's the driver of the black Lexus. The guy sits in a dark corner smoking his corncob pipe. We get a clear look at him for the first time. Short, chubby, not especially threatening. Davis says it was a mistake to take out so many kids at once. "Eight drunk teenagers is one thing. Twenty kids in a bus is something else." The driver bites his lip. Explains that he wired the wrong bus. The one he intended to wire was the equipment bus, which was occupied only by two team managers and a water boy.

"Don't let it happen again," says Davis curtly.

"Be careful who you're talking to," says the driver.

Davis glares at the driver, then apologizes.

Various burials, church services, memorials.

Clancy at school with Tish and Ozzie. They're talking about the deaths of the band members. "Least it wasn't the football team," says Ozzie. "I mean who gives a crap about half-time shows anyway?"

Clancy at work. Washing windows. Grace, Davis's mother, approaches Clancy. They have a pleasant chat about the fact that Davis is dating his mother. Clancy makes it clear he's happy about that. Grace says she looks forward to meeting her.

Clancy and Tish are at a grocery store picking up stuff for his mother. They run into Zack. They go for coffee. Zack tells how he did some work for Davis, then remarks on how much business Devonshire is getting since they took over. Zack then says that it doesn't seem natural. "Isn't it kind of weird how as soon as Devonshire Mortuaries comes to town people start dying? And twenty-nine of them were students."

"Coincidence," says Clancy.

"Twenty-nine deaths isn't coincidence; it's a plan," says Zack.

"What are you implying?" asks Clancy.

"It does seem a little odd, now that you mention it," says Tish. "The only high school age kids I remember croaking in the last ten years are that anorexic chick, the doofus who hung himself because he didn't get accepted at Harvard and the jock who ran himself over with the snowblower."

"What do you think's happening?" jokes Clancy. "That somebody's killing kids to get business?"

"Sure seems strange that all these teenagers are buying the farm," says Zack.

Later. Tish and Clancy discuss Zack's theory. Clancy thinks it's ridiculous. Tish thinks there's something to it.

Next day. At work. Clancy goes to Davis and brings up what Zack said about so many kids dying since Devonshire Mortuaries opened. Davis takes the question in stride. Gives Clancy a bullshit remark.

Later. Davis has a meeting with the Lexus driver. Points out that his concern about having so many band members die at once is now a problem. The upshot of the scene is that a couple of adults have to be taken care of. Davis says he already has one person in mind. He takes out the piece of paper with Walt Jeffries's name written on it. "Find two more in the usual way."

Neighborhood bar. Mainly retired guys drinking beer and bullshitting to pass the time. The black Lexus is parked outside. The driver sits at a table, checking things out. He notices one old-timer with thick horn-rimmed glasses engaged in conversation, ignoring his drink. Driver rises, passes the old guy with glasses and slips some powder into his beer.

Local YMCA. Black Lexus parked outside. A handful of elderly women are in an aerobics class. The locker room. The driver is picking the lock on a locker. Opens it. Looks for something. Can't find it. Picks another lock. Looks for something. Can't find it. He hits paydirt with the next locker. Inside a woman's purse with several vials of medication. Driver makes a switch.

A house. Mailbox in the front yard says JEFFRIES. The black Lexus pulls up. From inside the driver notices Walt puttering in the garden in the backyard. He lowers the passenger side window. Raises the same dart gun he used on the punk kid. Gets Walt in his sights, then fires.

Walt clutches his neck. But—IT'S NOT WALT JEFFRIES. Actually, it is. It's Walt's <u>father, WALT JEFFRIES SR</u>. Turns out they live together.

Later. The elderly woman from the YMCA is taking the medication that was switched. She keels over. Then we see the old guy who was poisoned at the bar lying dead on his kitchen

floor. Later. Walt Senior and Walt Junior are
having dinner, talking about the fact that
Beth is dating the new Funeral Director in
town. Then, like the skinhead before, Walt's
dad can't breathe. Clutches his head.
Screams. Convulses. Dies.

Walt calls Clancy's mom for moral support.
Walt's confused. His dad just had a physical. In perfect health. Walt orders an autopsy, which reveals the dart wound and
poison in the body. Now Walt knows somebody
murdered his dad. He calls up Davis to make
funeral arrangements. When Walt shows up,
Davis is shocked. He realizes the wrong Walt
Jeffries was killed.

MEANWHILE—Walt tells Beth that someone
murdered his father. She tells Clancy. And
Clancy innocently tells Davis.

Davis is concerned. He has a staff meeting. "A costly mistake has been made. Now we
have a cop snooping around."

The poisoned woman's and man's bodies are
in different viewing rooms at Devonshire
Mortuaries. So is Walt's father. Walt arrives. Receives visitors. Beth and Clancy
show up. Clancy is kind and supportive to
Walt.

Zack shows up to pay his respects to
Walt's dad. Notices the two other bodies.
Clancy and Zack fall into conversation.
Clancy says, "See, you're wrong. You said
only teenagers were dying. These three peo-
ple aren't teenagers."

Zack shrugs. "Let's see how old the next batch is."

Walt joins Clancy and Zack. Clancy excuses himself. Zack then shares his theory about all the young people dying with Walt.

It gets Walt thinking. He decides to investigate all the deaths that have happened since Devonshire Mortuaries came to town. He proceeds to examine the death certificates of the 29 teens, as well as the two elderly people who died.

MEANWHILE—Davis and Beth continue dating. And Ozzie keeps seeing Assistant Mary. He brings her to school on Career Day for a show-and-tell assignment. His horny classmates drool over Mary. Ozzie and Mary also expand their erotic trysts by screwing at night in the cemetery outdoors. He shows her the mausoleum clubhouse. While they are there, Clancy and Tish show up. Mary gets along with them. She tells Clancy how much Davis likes him. Tish asks questions about Devonshire Mortuaries. Mary claims to know nothing.

Back to Walt's investigation. None of the deceased except his father had an autopsy. Both of the older victims were assumed to have had heart attacks and all the dead teens were assumed to have either drowned or died in the bus explosion. The only death that stands out is the skinhead. By law he should've been autopsied, but his father had connections in city government, so none was done.

Walt gets a court order to have the skin-head's body exhumed. An autopsy is performed and the same dart wound and poison are discovered. Walt then orders the two elderly victims exhumed and autopsied. Sure enough, poison is found in both bodies.

Walt puts two and two together and decides that Zack's theory about Devonshire Mortuaries has enormous validity. Walt stops by Clancy's house, speaks briefly to Beth, saying that even though it's none of his business, she should stay away from Davis Crawley. He's a bad guy. Then Walt leaves.

Walt pays a visit to Davis. Confronts him. Davis is cool, tells him to prove it. They argue. Suddenly, out of nowhere comes the Lexus driver. Hits Walt on the head, knocking him out. Davis asks why the driver didn't just kill Walt. Driver says Walt's dying won't look good. "Let's disappear him," says the driver.

First Walt's police cruiser is hidden in the garage with the hearses. Then, we're in a viewing room. The body of a middle-aged woman in a coffin is being removed; then, STILL ALIVE BUT UNCONSCIOUS, Walt is placed at the bottom of the coffin, duct tape on his mouth and his hands and feet bound. Then the other body is placed back in the coffin, on top of Walt.

A funeral in progress. The coffin containing Walt and the dead woman is lowered into the ground. Grave diggers fill in the grave.

Later. Inside the coffin. Walt regains consciousness. He has no idea where he is but can't breathe. He manages to free his hands. Reaches into his jacket for his small flashlight. Turns it on. Still not sure where he is. Filled with adrenaline, he manages to push off the dead woman and then realizes where he is.

The terror and futility of his situation overwhelm him.

Walt's eyes bulge in utter horror at his fate.

That night Davis and the Lexus driver dump Walt's police cruiser into the river, the same one where the drunken teens drowned. Davis and the driver drive back in the Lexus. Davis is nervous. The driver says, "Relax; nothing can be traced back to us. Circumstantially, we're the only ones benefiting from all these people dying, but nobody can prove anything." He lights his corncob pipe.

Meanwhile, the small police force of the town (four men) is concerned. Walt's disappeared. Beth is called. She hasn't seen him. She's worried. She said the last thing he said to her was to stay away from Davis. Clancy says Walt only said that because he's jealous, but Beth said that there was such sincerity in his voice.

Clancy thinks about this and Zack's theory and Walt's disappearance. He bounces if off Tish. She says, "We need to find out more about Devonshire Mortuaries." They go to her computer and onto the Internet and Search for Devonshire Mortuaries. They find out that the company's five years old and that they specialize in buying failing funeral homes.

They also learn that Devonshire Mortuaries only goes into certain geographic areas. Tish punches in the areas. Florida. Oregon. Oklahoma. Wisconsin. Maine. There doesn't seem to be any rhyme or reason why they choose an area. Tish searches some more, then hits paydirt. Devonshire Mortuaries only goes into areas with a large population of baby boomers with children of high school age.

Further searching generates a theory: Devonshire buys a failing funeral home, renovates it, shows huge profits by killing to get a big volume of business. There's an unlimited supply of teenagers to draw from. Devonshire then resells it to an individual who wants to run an independent operation. The new owner thinks the modernized home will be a moneymaker based on the volume in the sales offering. Only now, without benefit of murder, the normal, slow influx of bodies occurs and the profits are minimal to nonexistent. So the new owners are screwed and Devonshire has moved on.

Clancy still can't believe it. Tish does.

He says he'll be convinced if he can somehow get a look at Davis's records. Clancy waits for a night when Davis and his mother are on a date. As Clancy works at Devonshire, he has a key, so he and Tish sneak in.

They go to Davis's office. After some difficulty, they find spreadsheets on the computer and—sure enough—they find the projected earnings game plan for the next two years listing the next areas in the country Devonshire is going to, as well as profit statements since the business began.

Clancy now realizes it's all true. He figures Walt must've found out and that Davis killed him. Clancy's immediate concern is for his mother's safety.

Tish tells him to get to his house. She'll stay behind and make a disk copy of the stuff they just saw on the computer screen. Clancy doesn't want to leave Tish alone. She insists. "It'll take five minutes. Make sure your mom's okay; then come back. I'll be outside." He takes off, speeds to his house. Davis's car is parked in the drive. Clancy approaches the house slowly. Peeks in the window and sees Davis and Beth making out on the living room couch. He recoils as Davis moves his hand up Beth's skirt. Clancy freaks. He rushes through the front door, breaking the mood.

Davis and Beth let go of each other. Clancy acts as if he doesn't know anything. There's an awkwardness; then Davis says he'd

better go. He says good-bye to Clancy. Beth
says she'll walk Davis to his car. Clancy
watches from the window. At the car Davis
and Beth kiss passionately.

Davis leaves. Beth returns to the house.
Clancy tells her everything. She doesn't believe him.

BACK TO TISH—Alone in the dark in Davis's
office. She's having trouble copying a disk.
She tries again. Then, in the darkness we
see the familiar corncob pipe. The DRIVER'S
VOICE says, "Having fun, young lady?"

Tish looks up. Scared.

"Does your mother know where you are?"
says the driver, still in the darkness. He
picks up the phone. Dials a number.

Davis in his car. Cell phone rings. He answers it. We hear the driver's voice on the
other end say, "Get your ass over here now."

Nervous, Davis floors it.

Clancy's house. He tells his mother to
call the cops and tell them to get over to
Devonshire Morticians. He wonders where Tish
is. Sensing she's in danger, he jumps in his
car and heads back to Devonshire.

Davis pulls into the parking lot. Rushes
into the home, then into his office. The
lights are on now. Sitting at his desk is
Tish.

Then we see the corncob pipe. And as the
person smoking it takes a puff we see that
the tip of his left index finger is missing.

But this person isn't the Lexus driver—

It's Grace, Davis's mother.

Only she's <u>not</u> his mother. She's his <u>father</u>! Dad likes to dress up in women's clothes.


ACT THREE

In a fit of rage Grace slaps Davis several times, verbally berating him, but in a <u>male voice</u>. He takes the abuse like a little boy. Tish is weirded out by hearing the deep male voice coming out of the "sweet, elderly Grace."

Davis and "Grace" argue about whose fault their predicament is. He says it's "hers" because she blew up the wrong bus. "She" says it's his for not knowing there was a Walt Jeffries <u>Sr</u>. "That's what got Walt Junior snooping around."

They go back and forth; then finally, Davis says there's no point in screaming. They have to put their heads together and solve the problem just like they always do.

Grace says she's already solved the problem. She says that people are going to think that they had caused all the deaths in order to make money. "There's only one way to prove to people that we're innocent."

"What's that?" says Davis.

"Somebody from our ranks has to die," she says. "If <u>we</u> lost someone, we'd be completely above suspicion."

"Who's it gonna be?" says Davis.

"I've already decided," says Grace. "<u>You</u>."

Then, before he can react, Grace pulls out a <u>different-looking</u> dart gun. "It'll be instantaneous. I put in three times the usual formula." She fires, hitting Davis in the left eye. He rushes toward "her," pulling her to the floor with him. In the process, Grace's wig falls off.

"Mom," says Davis as he dies.

Grace looks at Tish. "Now . . . what do I do with you?" she muses, a menacing look on her face. She puts her wig back on.

Clancy speeds along a road. When he gets to Devonshire he breathes a sigh of relief: Two police cars and an ambulance are there. He runs inside expecting to see Tish, but instead he sees—

"Grace" in tears, being comforted by Assistants Tom, Dick, Harry and Mary, all of whom are crying. Davis's dead body, sprawled across his desk, is being checked out by a Medical Examiner.

<u>There's no sign of Tish.</u>

Grace puts on a magnificent act for the cops and Medical Examiner. Here's her story: She heard a noise, came downstairs and found Davis collapsed on his desk. "He had a weak heart. He was always working. He cared so much. And with the huge amount of burials we've had since we opened, it must've been too much for his heart to take."

Clancy asks where Tish is. Nobody knows what he's talking about. He says he left her here. Grace says no one was here "but my son." Clancy's getting scared. He starts spewing out everything: Zack's theory, the data he and Tish found on the Internet, the marketing scheme of Devonshire Mortuaries and so on. He says Walt knew what was going on and that they killed him. Grace and her assistants all play dumb.

The cops think Clancy's losing his mind. One of them, who knows Zack, refers to him as "a drunk" with a wild imagination. Because the cops don't believe him, Clancy's a basket case. The Medical Examiner orders an autopsy on Davis. He and the cops leave with Davis's corpse.

Clancy says he's not leaving until he finds out where Tish is. Grace smiles at him, then before he knows it delivers a karate chop, knocking him out. "Put him with the girl." Assistants Tom and Dick carry Clancy away.

Assistant Harry asks Grace if the pathologist doing the autopsy will find anything. Grace says no because her special formula is laced with formaldehyde and, since formaldehyde is part of a mortician's life, they'll dismiss it. Assistant Mary asks what's going to happen to Clancy and Tish.

"We're going to make them disappear," says Grace.

"In the ground?" asks Mary.

"Up in smoke," says Grace.

CUT TO—The crematorium. Grace is turning on the heat. In another room, Tish and Clancy are tied up. He's still unconscious.

She's trying to wake him. In the coffin selection room, a cheap pine coffin is being removed by Assistants Dick and Harry. Back to Clancy and Tish. He starts to come to. "What's going on?" he asks. "I don't know," says Tish. But she tells him how Grace killed Davis. Tish also says that Grace is a man.

Before Clancy can absorb that last comment, Assistants Tom and Dick arrive and grab them.

We next see them being stuffed into the pine coffin, lying side by side. From their POV they see Assistants Tom and Dick sliding the lid onto the coffin. For a brief moment they also see Grace and Assistant Mary looking down.

The coffin lid is nailed shut. A crematory oven door is opened. The coffin is placed onto a platform and mechanically guided inside. Assistant Harry closes the door.

Grace and the assistants all leave.

Inside the coffin with Clancy and Tish. Because their hands and feet are tied and there's hardly enough room to move, there's not much they can do.

Devonshire office. Grace pulls Assistant Tom aside and tells him that since Davis is gone, he will be the new Head Funeral Director. "You're like a son to me," says Grace.

Cut back and forth from inside and outside the coffin as the flames slowly begin to engulf the coffin. Smoke starts to fill the coffin. Assistant Dick asks Assistant Harry if he feels like going out for a drink. They leave.

The coffin. It's filling up with smoke. The pine is burning. Flames are coming through. Tish has passed out. Clancy's about to drift away, but then—

Suddenly, the lid is yanked off. A hand reaches in!

It's ASSISTANT MARY.

She helps Clancy out; then he lifts Tish out. He has a few burn marks here and there, but he's all right. In a quick conversation, Mary says that she just couldn't stand seeing all the young people dying. She explains that Grace is indeed a man, a mortician who came up with a scam. He would find troubled teens, take them under his wing, raise them as his own children and train them to be assistants. He had operations like this all over the country.

Mary's final comment: "Grace has to be stopped. So does all the killing. Call the police." Clancy says they won't believe him. Mary says they will if he brings Grace to them.

The story builds to a confrontation between Clancy and Grace. But before that happens, Clancy has to fend off Davis's replacement—Assistant Tom, who's loyal to Grace. They have a fight that makes lots of noise, alerting Grace. Mary again comes to Clancy's aid by knocking out Tom. They lock him in the deep freeze, where bodies are kept on ice.

But Mary's leg was injured. She can't help Clancy anymore. He must face Grace alone. This happens with a violent confrontation that winds up in the embalming room. In their struggle, Clancy manages to tear off Grace's wig and rip part of his dress, revealing the padding and whatnot that make him look like a woman.

Because he's a man, Grace easily overpowers Clancy, primarily by throwing formaldehyde onto Clancy's burns. In horrible pain, Clancy is weakened. Grace straps him to an embalming table. She's going to embalm him— <u>alive</u>.

As Grace prepares a solution of embalming fluid, "she" rants and raves about the baby-boomer generation. "The only thing the baby boomers did well was fuck. They made lots of kids. And most of you little bastards are worthless, disrespectful, self-centered pricks."

As Grace carries on, Clancy notices an embalmer's tool. (NOTE: Earlier, in the scene with Ozzie and Mary, we saw several tools of the trade.) Clancy grabs it, lashes out, cuts Grace's face. He also manages to cut himself free.

Another struggle and at the last minute again Grace gets the better of Clancy. Grace is about to kill him when out of nowhere <u>an-</u>

other sharp-edged embalming tool is shoved
into Grace's back and through her chest.
Grace dies.

Holding the tool is—Ozzie.

"Got here as fast as I could," he says,
then explains that Mary telephoned him asking for help.

### EPILOGUE

Clancy visiting Tish in her hospital room.
He tells her he doesn't want to be a Funeral
Director anymore. All that they've been
through has cured him of his morbid fascination with death.

Ozzie is visiting Mary in jail. We learn
that even though she didn't personally kill
anyone, she knew what was going on, so she's
an accessory. But because she saved Clancy
and Tish and helped put an end to Grace her
sentence will be lenient: six months in jail
and probation.

Ozzie and Clancy stand before the Devonshire Mortuaries sign. Ozzie says, "My mom's
the town lesbian and I'm dating a mortician
who's a jailbird. Not good for the image."

Fade out on the Devonshire Mortuaries sign
being removed and a new sign replacing it:

Coming Soon
A New
International House of Pancakes

Registered WGA East by D. B. Gilles

A final word on treatments. Know how to write them, but it's more important to your career as a screenwriter to know how to write a screenplay. Don't rely on getting deals with your treatments. There's nothing an agent, manager, producer, or studio likes better than a completed script.

What I can't emphasize enough, though, is the importance of knowing what your story is and where it's going.

Make sure you have your story down and you won't get lost.

## Assignment

Do an outline, three-act story line, or (if you're feeling courageous) a treatment for the screenplay you want to write.

Suggestion: If you're unclear on where the act breaks fall, follow the format of *Growl* (see pages 99–103), *then* try the three-act story line following the format of *Midnight Snack* (see page 104–109).

# Not Yet!

I know you want to start writing
your screenplay, but wait.
More stuff has to be covered.

## Colloquium

# The Well-Made Screenplay

Writing is the hardest work in the world. I have been
a bricklayer and a truck driver, and I tell you—as if you
haven't been told a million times already—
that writing is harder. Lonelier. And nobler and more enriching.
—HARLAN ELLISON

Long before there were screenplays there were screen *plays*. Check out movies from the thirties. You'll see a credit that separates the words "screen" and "play."

Screen Play
by
Whoever

Although it looks awkward now, it seemed like the logical description back then. Somewhere along the line the two words were blended. It's easy to understand why, in the early days of the movie business, they would separate the two words.

Two thousand years before there were films there were plays. In the beginning of the film industry, they called movies moving pictures, and when sound was added they were called talkies.

Before the talkies there were the silent films, which enraptured my grandparents and your great-great-great(?)-grandparents because up to that point there were no movies. For entertainment, people went to the theater. And theater was a luxury, primarily for the well off and educated. Which is what was so democratic about silent films. They were accessible and affordable to pretty much everybody.

Which takes us back to the nineteenth century, when something called the well-made play came into existence.

The well-made play is the precursor to screenplays as we know them today. In most books about screenwriting the concept of the three-act structure is emphasized. The first act should end with a problem that must be solved by the hero. The second act is filled with obstacles that prevent the hero from getting what he wants, building to an event at the end of Act Two that propels the hero in a final quest to achieve what he has sought or in an unexpected direction in which he must find something else. Act Three builds to the hero either attaining or not attaining what he has been searching for, presumably resulting in a satisfying conclusion for the audience.

If you've ever wondered where this structure came from—

## A Brief History of the Well-Made Play

The well-made play is constructed according to strict technical principles that produce neatness of plot and theatrical effectiveness.

It was developed around 1825 by a French playwright named Eugène Scribe and became dominant on nineteenth-century stages in the United States and Europe. It called for complex, artificial plotting, a buildup of suspense, a climactic scene in which all problems are resolved, and a happy ending.

Says Mr. Scribe:

*You go to the theatre not for instruction or correction, but for relaxation and amusement. Now, what amuses you most is not truth but fiction. To represent what is before your very eyes every day is not the way to please you; but what does not come to you in your usual life, the extraordinary, the romantic, that is what charms you. That is what one is eager to offer you.*

Maybe a little wordy, but he has a point.

Scribe went on to create a five-act structure, although he was most likely inspired by a Greek playwright or two and another Frenchman, Pierre Corneille, himself credited with introducing what has become a stock character, that of the flirtatious young girl, usually a minor female role, typically a lady's maid. (More about this in a bit.)

## The Five-Act Play Structure

**Act One:** Mainly expository and lighthearted. Toward the end of the act, the antagonists are engaged and the conflict is initiated.

**Acts Two and Three:** The action fluctuates in an atmosphere of mounting tension from good fortune to bad.

**Act Four:** The stage is generally filled with people and there is an outburst of some kind—a scandal, a quarrel, a challenge. At this point, things usually look pretty bad for the hero. The climax is in this act.

**Act Five:** Everything is worked out logically so that in the final scene the cast assembles and reconciliations take place and there is an equitable distribution of prizes in accordance with poetic justice and reinforcing the morals of the day. Everyone leaves the theater content.

Mr. Scribe wrote many plays and applied his techniques to a variety of genres: comedies, tragedies, fantasies, historical plays, even operas, but mostly to plays of contemporary life in order that the plays be topical or at least seem to be topical.

His plays were taken from the French headlines of the day. They were aimed—as their modern counterparts are today—at the tastes of the newly semieducated middle class, who were the products of the national school university systems set up by Napoléon. By their very nature, these plays became dated quickly, though their structures remain durable enough to warrant imitation.

### The Formal Characteristics of the Well-Made Play

1. The play follows a strict logic of cause and effect.
2. The plot is based on a secret known to the audience and withheld from the major characters so as to be revealed to them in a climactic scene.
3. The plot usually describes the culmination of a long story, most of which has happened before the start of the play. This late point of attack requires that the audience be informed of the antecedent material in exposition in the form of dialogue or monologue. Scribe frequently used soliloquies and asides.
4. Action and suspense grow more intense as the play proceeds. This rise in intensity is arranged in a pattern achieved by the contrivance of entrances, exits, letters, revelations of identity, and other such devices.
5. The protagonist, in conflict with an adversary, experiences alternately good and bad turns of fortune. This creates the emotional rhythm of the play.
6. The lowest point in the hero's fortune occurs just before the highest. The latter occurs in an obligatory scene that characteristically hinges on the disclosure of secrets.
7. The plot, or part of it, is frequently knotted by a misunderstanding, a quid pro quo, in which a word or situation is understood in opposite ways by two or more characters.
8. The denouement—literally, the "untying"—(the resolution) is logical and clear. It's not supposed to have any loose ends to confuse the audience.

9. The overall action pattern of the play is reproduced on a small scale in each act. It is, in fact, the principle according to which each minor climax and scene is constructed.

By the end of the nineteenth century and into the twentieth, Scribe's five-act structure evolved into a three-act structure. Most plays were in three acts. Is there any wonder that the American playwrights lured to Hollywood structured their screenplays into three acts? Over the last forty years, most plays tend to be in two acts.

But screenplays tend to be broken down into three acts.

Act One ends around page 30.

Act Two ends around page 82.

Act Three ends around page 110.

(Note: In the past, the page breakdowns of screenplays tended to have Act Two end at page 90 and Act Three at page 120, but over the last few years scripts have been getting shorter. I always tell my students to aim for a 110-page screenplay.)

I know of some screenwriting instructors and gurus who use the five-act structure (which is pretty much an expanded three-act structure).

Like this:

Act One ends around page 17.

Act Two ends around page 38.

Act Three ends around page 60.

Act Four ends around page 90.

Act Five ends around page 120.

If you're saying, "I want to write screenplays. Why do I need to know about the well-made play?" remember this: You want to be part of a long tradition of storytellers. It's an honorable profession.

As 2000 approached, do you remember who was named Man of the Millennium?

William Shakespeare.

A playwright.

A storyteller.

It's important that you know not only who came before you but also how they forged the rules that ultimately resulted in the art form you're choosing to work in.

When Hollywood was taking its baby steps in the 1920s and '30s, where did the studious go to find people to write movies?

Broadway.

Playwrights.

These men and women applied what they knew about writing plays to writing screen plays.

# Lecture 13

# To Make a Long Story Short

To go beyond is as wrong as to fall short.
—CONFUCIUS

Do you write nine sentences when one word will make your point? Do you use a three-page paragraph when a sentence would work just fine? Do you put down six pages when a short paragraph will suffice? Do you feel compelled to overstate your case? Do you repeatedly hit readers on the head to make sure they "get it"? Do you pile on so many inconsequential details and so much excessive information that you yourself are lost and confused in your own story?

If you're guilty of these and other uncontrollable urges to, well, write too much, you're an Overwriter. Being one doesn't mean there's a twelve-step program in your future, but if the shoe fits, you already know that your inability to decide what needs to be cut has hindered you.

If you still aren't sure whether or not you're an Overwriter, consider the following:

You know you're an Overwriter if you've read a few books on screenwriting and learned that screenplays should be no more than 120 pages, but yours comes in at 184 (but in an attempt to fool people you used a smaller typeface and font, so the script is really 239 pages).

You know you're an Overwriter when your head says, *End the scene,* but your heart says, *Put in the heroine's trip to Tuscany and the great fettuccine she ate the night she met the expatriate American chef who taught her about Northern Italian red wines.*

Overwriters can't stop themselves. And that's not such a bad thing, as long they know that once they've finished the first draft they have to take the gloves off and start cutting.

Overwriters can overcome their limitations—it's a matter of deciding what has to be eliminated.

## How Do You Know What Has to Go?

As a screenwriting teacher at New York University and elsewhere I've read nearly fifteen hundred screenplays. The one sure thing I've seen again and again is that scripts come in either too long or too short. I've broken it down to percentages: 65 percent of the screenplays are overwritten, 25 percent are underwritten, and the remaining 10 percent come in at the right length.

I always ask my new students if they are Underwriters or Overwriters. Most of them don't know what they are because they haven't written enough to find out. But by the time they've turned in their first writing assignment I know and they know. Without fail, my 65/25/10 percent equation applies. Of course, besides an overlong screenplay, there are usually other problems that need to be dealt with, but right now I'm concentrating on screenplays that are too long.

The first mistake an Overwriter makes is not following the guidelines.

Each year I am asked to read a number of scripts sent in by applicants to the Graduate Program of the Department of Dramatic Writing. Following my 65 percent theory, I always look for the thickest manuscripts just to see how right I am.

The most egregious screenplay submission I ever saw was 443 pages. It was the equivalent of four normal-sized screenplays. I had to read it. In all candor, I was predisposed to dislike it before I read the first word, not because of the content but because of the length.

Just by looking at it I knew the author didn't do his homework. A script for a four-hour miniseries is half as long as this tome was. The author submitted a screenplay for what he perceived was a historical epic spanning one hundred years in the life of one family.

There are numerous books on the market with information on formatting a screenplay. He didn't appear to have read, or even thumbed through, any of them. If he did, he chose to ignore the information. Before I read the first page I already knew the script would have huge problems. And it did. The end result was that I did not recommend that the person be accepted into the program. That author's basic problem was an inability to recognize how much his readers needed to know and when they needed to know it.

## How Much Do We Need to Know and When Do We Need to Know It?

What Overwriters need to learn is that we don't have to know everything about a character, especially the main character, right away. Overwriters reveal too much too soon. Readers get bogged down in Protagonist Information Overkill. It's okay to find out bits and pieces as we go along, with a few surprises along the way.

For example, in a new friendship and especially in a new romance, we learn things gradually. I don't know about you, but I get uncomfortable when I encounter people who give too much information about themselves too soon. I feel as if I'm being forced to absorb too many details before I can decide if I want to get to know someone better.

An overwritten scene is like a conversation with a stranger (or someone we barely know) that goes on too long. If someone is giving us too much information, sharing too much, saying too much, crossing boundaries, and getting too personal, telling us more than we ever needed or wanted to know about her or her kids or her dog, it becomes a turnoff.

The same Information Overkill applies to plot. Overwriters take forever to start telling their story. They get bogged down in the details and minutiae of time, place, mood, setup, situation, language—whatever. They lose sight of the value of introducing the slimmest thread of plot reasonably soon. Mysteries are perfect examples of getting a story started right away. Check out David Lynch's *Blue Velvet,* in which the discovery of a severed human ear occurs quite fast, or Woody Allen's *Crimes and Misdemeanors,* where Martin Landau comes upon a letter to his wife from his mistress.

There's nothing wrong with giving the reader a hint of "what's going on?" or "what's this thing about?" reasonably soon, say five to nine pages into a screenplay (rather than fifty-eight).

So whether it's in a screenplay or in life, the big question is what, and how much, do I reveal at the beginning (the first date, the first lunch, the first day on the new job, the first day at the new club)?

This is the easy part.

One of the first tools of writing a journalism student is introduced to is the Rule of the Inverted Pyramid. This is a clever device in which the most important details of a news story should be in the first paragraph, working downward to the least important.

In all forms of fiction, the opposite is true. Save the best detail for last. Always aim for the unexpected surprise, the huge revelation, the big finish.

This is not to say that you should be sparse with the information you provide at the beginning. The first few pages is where you must hook the reader. So give your character her best shot as soon as we meet her, even if she's supposed to be evil or nasty. Make us want to spend time with her. Make us want to know what makes her tick. Simply put, reveal information gradually.

The old saying "You only get one chance to make a first impression" applies just as much to a script as it does to a person. No agent, producer, or Development Executive will read your script twice. If they aren't grabbed by the first few pages, they won't read the rest. There are too many screenplays piling up on their desks to waste their time on yours.

In my Comedy Writing Workshop at NYU I tell students that the most important page of their script is the first page. If there aren't any laughs on page 1, an agent or TV producer may not bother reading the remaining forty-seven pages. This also applies to a screenplay that's a comedy. Cram as many laughs as you can onto the first page.

I'm not sure when I heard the word "backstory" for the first time. It was probably uttered by a Hollywood producer or Development Executive, but that was a moment that was to change my life as both a writer and a teacher.

"Backstory" is a peculiar term that encompasses where the protagonist presumably has been, what he's been through, and how he has handled the slings and arrows of his life.

He is then placed into a dramatic situation that, in all likelihood, he is unprepared for (because of his backstory) or incredibly prepared for (because of his backstory), but he must learn that he isn't as ready for the dramatic situation as he thought. For example, in the film adaptation of James Dickey's *Deliverance,* there are two examples of each. Because more people have probably seen the movie than read the book, I'll refer to the actors playing the roles.

Jon Voight played Ed, a tentative, nonaggressive guy who goes on a fishing trip to a remote and dangerous river that winds through a wilderness that also turns out to have hidden dangers. Although by no means a wimp, his character is the most soft-spoken and gentle of the four men.

Leading the fishing expedition is Lewis, played by Burt Reynolds. This guy is your basic supermacho alpha-male, hairy-chested Ernest Hemingway wannabe. Now, relating this movie to "backstory," Burt Reynolds's character's backstory has prepared him to be in the middle of a dangerous, remote wilderness and to be able to survive. He's a hunter, fisherman, archer, river rafter. This experience should be a real piece of cake for him.

Then he breaks his leg in a freak accident and is unconscious. One of the other four guys is missing and the third, because of something horrible that has happened to him, is pretty much ineffectual.

Who must save the day? Jon Voight. The least prepared of the bunch.

So after overcoming all obstacles, including being forced to kill a man (and we've learned early on that Voight has a problem killing things, because he was unable to shoot an arrow at a deer), he survives and saves his two friends. Now on to the key questions: How much of a character's backstory does the reader need to know? In what stages should the writer release that information?

I say the screenplay should give us a clear picture of the character's major flaw, then pull back. Start telling your story and provide a few more details, but hold off on the really juicy stuff. Make us really like the guy. Make us feel for him. Make us think we really have a handle on him.

Then throw us a curveball and give us something big at the end of the script.

Isn't that what happens in the dating game? Everything's going just fine with your new romance. He's charming, funny, a good dancer, considerate, and isn't afraid to reveal a couple of personal things about himself that might tarnish his image: (1) He goes to Gamblers Anonymous but hasn't placed a bet in four years. (2) He gets kind of depressed once in a while, but he takes a little blue pill every day that perks him up. (3) He spent a night in jail once, but it was when he was in college and got in a bar fight with a rival fraternity.

These three bits of his backstory might turn off some women, but others might find him appealing because he's been so forthright. Other than for these little peccadilloes, he's a pretty good catch.

Then about seven weeks into the relationship he casually reveals that he has been married. When the woman asks why he didn't bring it up before, he explains that it didn't seem important because the marriage was years ago and he seldom even thinks about it. Information that is still understandable and forgivable.

About ten weeks into the relationship, after the woman inquires one night about his first wife and asks the innocent question, "How long have you been divorced?" he responds, "We didn't get divorced."

"You're still married?" asks the woman in shock.

"Actually, no," he responds, then casually explains that his first wife killed herself. He came home one day and found her hanging in the closet.

This is not the kind of backstory or information that should be revealed on the first date. The time must be right. And in the ongoing drama of a new romance if something as tragic as that is told too soon, it could easily bring things to an immediate end. (Incidentally, this is a true story. My friend stopped dating the guy immediately.)

If in the beginning scenes of a screenplay about the preceding scenario the man told the woman about his wife's suicide, it's just too overwhelming a piece of information to handle. Not only for the female, who would certainly have to think twice about seeing the guy again, but for the reader, too.

It's information that's a surprise, so make it have a payoff by revealing it well into the script.

Deciding what to reveal and not reveal about your main character is just the beginning of the editing process. There are other characters to be dealt with, as well as the main plot and subplots.

Constantly remind yourself that every aspect of your overlong first draft must be examined with a critical, objective eye.

- Do you need to say this?
- Have you already said it?
- Can you say it better?

- Is this character necessary?
- Does this subplot go anywhere?
- Is your protagonist filled with so many shadings and contours that you forgot who he is?
- Have you revealed too much?
- Have you revealed too much too soon?
- Have you written a fabulous payoff that resolves all the questions and problems introduced in your story and is followed by an additional seventy-five pages?
- Are you revealing so much that you don't know where you are in your own story?
- Is your story so overplotted and overwritten that you've overwhelmed even yourself?
- Does the sheer size of your manuscript scare you when you realize you have to wade through it?

At the end of the day, overwriting is a condition that may never be permanently cured, but it can be dealt with project by project.

Never forget, as R. Buckminster Fuller said nearly one hundred years ago, "less is more."

However, as you'll see in the next chapter, less is more isn't always necessarily good.

# Lecture 14

# Why Less Is More Isn't Always True

Every writer I know has trouble writing.
–JOSEPH HELLER

Just as some people talk too much and others don't say enough, it's the same with screenwriters. Some overdo it and, well, some underdo it.

These are the Underwriters, whom I mentioned briefly in the previous lecture.

How do you know if you're an Underwriter? It goes back to my 65/25/10 percent theory in the previous lecture.

If you're given an assignment that should be thirty pages, an Underwriter turns in nineteen.

Underwriters all love text messaging. Their e-mails never begin with a "Hi" or "Hello"—just a sentence—and half of the time they don't sign their name.

Underwriters have short messages on their answering machines. They love Post-its. They don't like their characters to talk much. Scenes that could run four pages end after one and a half. Their stage directions are few and far between.

Although reading an underdone screenplay takes less time, in order for a full-length screenplay to really be full-length, it has to be at least 100 pages. Even better is 105.

For some screenwriters, even getting to page 85 is a monumental task. But there are ways to get your script up to the industry standard length without unnecessarily padding it.

## Basic Rules for Underwriters

### Let Your Characters Talk

Characters should say only what they need to say to accomplish the objective of the scene.

This is where being an Underwriter comes in handy. Your dialogue tends to be lean and mean.

Unfortunately, it's probably so lean that there's no meat on the bone.

Underwriters tend to mistrust their dialogue. Let's say you're writing a romantic comedy. You start a two-character scene. It begins nicely. Key information that will further the plot is given. You get an idea that the guy should tell a funny story about how much he loves his dog. Because you assume it'll mean going off on a tangent you decide not to include it. That's where you make your mistake.

Let him talk.

Underwriters tend to begin a two- or three-character scene well, with nice, taut dialogue. It's just starting to build to some conflict that will turn up the heat and we're waiting for some explosives; then . . .

They end the scene.

Let your people talk!

### Don't Be Afraid of Stage Directions

Stage directions are rarely a problem for Underwriters. However, there are times when it might be helpful if you embellished the setup of a scene.

```
INT. KITCHEN-DAY
Sally sits at the table. The phone rings.
```

You could add *something* to give us a stronger sense of the moment.

```
INT. KITCHEN-DAY
Sally sits at the table staring nervously at
the telephone, sipping a cup of tea. Her
hand shakes as she raises the cup to her lips.
Suddenly, the phone rings, startling her.
```

Remember *never* to pad your script with obvious clutter. It's better to give a few more details and information that will help your screenplay become more fully realized.

- Embellish your lead character by giving her a smaller problem to solve in addition to the Major Dramatic Question.
- Introduce a new subplot that's organic to the story or a character. For example, your protagonist or her best friend has fingernails that continuously break. This is a problem because she's going to an important business meeting and wants her nails to look great. Don't just stick something in.
- Add a new character who will complement the main character's plight.
- Find additional complications and obstacles. In TV most sitcoms have an A story and a B story. Some shows have C and D stories. The C and D stories are smaller in import but nevertheless compelling to watch as they play out.

Not only is padding cheating, it's also easy to spot. You're not fooling anyone when you bulk up the description of somebody's living room or skip lots of spaces between the sentences in your action sequences.

## Colloquium

# The Conscious Mind Is the Last to Know

A neurosis is a secret that you
don't know you are keeping.
—KENNETH TYNAN

The conscious mind is the enemy of creativity and reality. It compels you to follow someone else's rules, be polite, and do what you think won't upset or offend people.

The title of this chapter, if interpreted from a psychological rather than creative point of view, refers to how we let ourselves deny that which is obvious to everyone else. For example:

- The girl whose boyfriend is cheating on her. Everybody knows but her.
- The parents whose son is gay. Everybody knows but them.
- The adult daughter whose mother is an alcoholic. Everybody knows but her.
- The person who is under the impression she has an agent in Hollywood because he told her how much he liked her script and that he wanted to represent her and she signed a contract, but he hasn't returned any of her calls for seven months. She doesn't have an agent. She still clings to the notion that she does. *Don't ask!*

There are many other examples of this kind of denial. We all do it in one way or another, to one degree or another. The conscious mind protects us from that which we fear has happened or will happen. The conscious mind also protects the creative side of our brains by not allowing us to let go and write what we really want to write, especially if it's not something safe and easy. This is especially true for young screenwriters. Let's say you're writing a scene between two sixteen-year-olds. You know how kids talk. Their dialogue can be filled with expletives and sexual references. But because you're fearful your mother or your teacher will be offended or upset by the fact that you're using rough (but real) language, you tone it down and make it nice and polite.

That's your conscious mind at work.

The art of self-censorship doesn't only apply to language. It can keep you from writing truthfully as well.

Let's say you've had experience with an alcoholic parent. You know the dark side. You know what it's like to wake up in the morning and find empty beer bottles on the kitchen table. Perhaps you want to write something about what it's like to be the teenage son of an alcoholic mother. You know you can write the scene in your sleep, but again, you're afraid of what people who read the material will think of you. Or your mother. You're fearful that they'll think you're writing about your mother. Even if you are, you're petrified that people will find out that your childhood wasn't as happy as you've led them to believe.

You can choose to not write the scene at all. Or you can tone it down and make it seem that your mother got drunk only occasionally. Or you can flip it and write the scene as if your mother was a teetotaler who got drunk *one* time and write about how funny that was. Ultimately, as a writer, you're looking for the emotional payoff your main character gets. And as a writer you're looking for the best way to have your main character experience that payoff.

When it comes to the conscious mind, it's all about you deciding how close to the bone you want to get.

Who wants to acknowledge something painful or uncomfortable in life, let alone in what they write?

Another way screenwriters give in to their conscious minds is by writing derivative material. It can show up as plots we've seen a million times, jokes we've heard, clichéd characters we're tired of, predictable storytelling, and uninspired endings.

True creativity comes only when you think about writing something in an unconventional manner.

When I say to avoid what's been done before, I'm not talking about the idea or premise of the film. Let's say you have an idea for a romantic comedy. Ultimately, the story will have to do with a boy and a girl winding up together at the end after overcoming all kinds of obstacles, and that's the way it should be.

When you reach for original material I'm talking about the story. I'm talking about the *way* you choose to tell that story. You can have clichéd, done-to-death characters everyone's tired of seeing or you can write about a character we haven't seen before.

You've heard the expression "Necessity is the mother of invention."

That's applicable to screenwriting as well. After you've churned out three or four screenplays that were safe in idea, safe in dialogue, and safe in execution because they were workmanlike at best, you wake up one morning with an idea unlike the kind you normally get. It may shock you. You might think, *I don't write stuff like this.* All the better. Write it down *immediately,* wherever you are. If you don't, you'll forget it. It'll evaporate as quickly as it appeared.

You've also heard the expression "Take the gloves off."

Sometimes in the screenwriting game it's necessary to take the gloves off creatively.

Instead of telling the story of the meek, shy, bookwormish high school girl who yearns to be a poet, write one about a sixteen-year-old girl whose father is in jail for armed robbery, whose mother makes ends meet by dancing at a topless bar, whose older sister is living with a coke dealer, and whose thirteen-year-old brother with ADD is a pyromaniac obsessed with Internet porn. By trying something over-the-top like this you'll test your imagination and you'll be entering dramatic territory that's most likely unfamiliar (and uncomfortable) for you.

Don't be afraid to write something you wouldn't normally write.

Don't be afraid to write something personal. Specifically, something you've been ashamed of and worried that people would find out about.

You may find yourself in different waters, but you'll also find a whole new source of writing possibilities.

# Lecture 15

# The Screenplay That Wouldn't End

I always know the ending;
that's where I start.
–TONI MORRISON

Endings are a problem for everyone. Not only for new screenwriters but also for seasoned pros. And not only for screenplays but for finished films, too. Studios have test screenings to make sure the film works as a whole and to find out if the ending is a crowd-pleaser.

Endings have been a problem for thousands of years. In the ancient Greek dramas the deus ex machina would sometimes descend from Olympus at the last moment and straighten out an apparently hopeless situation by superhuman means.

Oftentimes the playwright himself would employ a supernatural power to make his characters contradict their innate selves so the

If you don't know much about Greek drama, Google the words "Greek Drama." There are many sites, but one of the best is http://www.watson.org/~leigh/drama.html. What you find will be of enormous help to you as a storyteller. This site introduces you to the history, mythology, and philosophy of Greek drama and gives you additional links.

story might end happily. However, eleventh-hour changes of heart on the part of the hero or antagonist are big no-nos today. Such last-minute changes reek of amateurish writing and don't feel right for the character, either.

Avoid artificiality in your endings. As the saying on the street goes, "Keep it real."

Actions cannot be unmotivated and illogical. Don't tag on a happy ending when a darker resolution is more organic. As Shakespeare said, "Strong reasons make strong actions." In life we may wake up on some days without any kind of plan or agenda. We just go with the flow or do nothing but watch TV or read a book. There is no reason, big or small, to do anything.

But in your screenplay your main character must have something she wants. And the entire script must be about her attempts to get it. And if she gets it, you might further complicate things by having her realize she doesn't want it. Or by getting it she's faced with the problem that she wants more.

Another dilemma you face is how to not make your ending predictable.

Don't you hate it when you know how something's going to end? Part of the pleasure of going to a movie is being continually surprised all the way to the last seconds.

Even if it's a romantic comedy and you know that the boy and girl will get together, it's always more enjoyable if there's the slight possibility that they won't. A good example of unpredictability is *Sweet Home Alabama*. Check it out. It's not a particularly terrific romantic comedy, but it's well structured and keeps you guessing who Reese Witherspoon will choose.

Often, even with a solid outline or three-act story line, a screenwriter will find herself approaching the middle of Act Three with the horrible realization that the ending she *thought* would happen is no longer the right ending. This discovery could require going back and doing major adjustments, which might also shake the foundation of the story. On the other hand, those adjustments may also make the story work.

Rewriting is what will make your story better. The more you rewrite, the more you get in touch with your characters and the story you want to tell.

Worse, someone with an outline or solid three-act story line who didn't quite get a handle on how the story should end in the early stages finds herself with no logical, satisfactory way to end it.

You might think that if you're writing a whodunit you wouldn't have ending problems.

Not necessarily.

What if, as author, all along you had it in your head that Harvey the Plumber was the killer, but as the story progressed you realized having him be the killer was too obvious? So you had to decide on somebody else. Now, if you've been writing a character with the idea that she is a nice, sweet person—say Sister Mary Elizabeth, the cool nun with the sense of humor—and then you decide that *she* will be the killer, it's going to mean going back and doing some adjusting.

There are no easy fixes for scripts with troublesome endings. If there's one temporary solution, it's to go with what you've got just so you can finish the first draft. Even if it's a horribly wrong ending, you should get to it. The goal is to type the words "Fade Out. The End." Even if you say: "And then he got hit by his neighbor's SUV. Fade Out. The End." Do it.

Then go back and read the whole script and see what you've got. Somewhere in those pages you'll find the answer. If you don't, one of your trusted friends might. Sometimes your best critic is someone who brings nothing more than common sense to the task. The person isn't there to judge or praise, just to read and react with honesty. A person's age or education doesn't matter. Look for someone you *know* is a straight shooter.

## Completion Issues

Just as some screenwriters can't find the right ending, there are others who can't finish their script.

They keep writing and writing and writing.

Never ending is a common ailment. They're afraid to either finish something or send it out into the world. They're afraid of rejection. Or being told it's not good enough or not funny enough or not "whatever" enough. They're afraid to find out if they're resilient enough to be a screenwriter.

So they play it safe. They keep working on the same script endlessly, then put it away and start another one, then go back to the first, do more work on it, then go back to the second and maybe finish it, then start a third.

This is a problem. Finishing a script (and in my book that means doing a number of drafts until it's officially finished and ready to be sent to agents and producers) is hard enough. But not getting an answer—one way or another—is even harder.

I'd rather finish a script, get it out there, have twenty agents say, "No thanks," or twenty producers say, "No thanks," and put it away than never know. If it gets turned down, the script has had its time at bat. That's all you want. Let the script get seen. If everyone turns it down, so be it. Then go on to the next one.

Just because your script gets turned down doesn't mean it's a bad screenplay. There are other reasons, out of your control. And you will always have that script. When the day comes that you sell another one and you're suddenly hot, that's when you pull that first one out of the proverbial drawer and let it have another shot.

Don't be afraid. As the saying goes, "The greatest risk is not taking one."

## Lecture 16

# Finding Your Voice: Comedy

Analyzing humor is like dissecting a frog. Few people are
interested and the frog dies of it.

–E. B. WHITE

Was there a moment in your life when you acknowledged to yourself that you were funny? Maybe you were *trying* to be funny. Maybe you weren't. Maybe it just slipped out.

Somebody laughed.

It might have happened when you were in second grade, a freshman in high school, a senior in college, or out of school and into a career.

Somebody laughed.

You liked saying funny things. Maybe you even loved it. Getting laughs did something to you. Maybe it built up your confidence. Made you feel cool. Hip. So you kept at it and you reached the point where you *knew* you were funny. Then one day it hit you.

You were watching a lousy sitcom or a mediocre *Saturday Night Live* sketch or you'd just laid out some hard-earned bucks at your local cineplex for a comedy that sucked. Then, as if possessed by the ghost of Groucho Marx, you thought or uttered seven words that would change your life:

"I could write funnier stuff than that."

Once you've made that statement, you'll face one important question: How do I go about doing it?

That's when you'll hit your first brick wall. Could you *really* write funnier stuff than that? You'd never tried to write anything funny before.

Not for real.

Maybe in high school or college you channeled your comedic ability into a satirical essay for an English class or you dashed out a humor column for the school paper. You might've written a couple of skits for a school talent show.

But you never, *not ever,* tried to write a sketch on the level of *Saturday Night Live*'s best or a spec script for an episode of your favorite sitcom.

Let's get real: You definitely never wrote a joke. The only jokes you told were the ones you heard from other people, just like everyone else. But to actually write an *original* joke? Maybe you could spontaneously *say* funny stuff, but to *write* funny stuff? To do that meant you were in entirely different waters.

As for screenwriting? No *way* you even thought about that. You? Writing a comedy that could fill 110 pages?

Then one morning you wake up and decide to give comedy writing a shot. You narrow it down to the form you feel will be the best fit. Stand-up? No. That involves performing. Sketch writing? With only a handful of venues on the tube, you know there aren't that many opportunities to break in. Besides, writing sketches isn't your thing. As for sitcoms, you realize that you don't watch many of them other than *Seinfield* reruns and *The Simpsons* and, of course, *Curb Your Enthusiasm* (but you know Larry David doesn't require your services).

All that's left is screenwriting. Deep down, being a screenwriter is what you thought about being more than anything. You enjoy movies more than TV. And you prefer comedies to everything else.

So you're ready to start. But you're nervous, maybe even a little intimidated and scared. That's natural. It'll pass.

After you overcome the fear of whether or not you *can* write a funny screenplay, how do you begin?

Start by renting comedies, and not just from the last few years. Go back to when the movie industry began. Check out the great comedians of the silent era, starting with Charlie Chaplin, Buster Keaton, and Fatty Arbuckle, then work your way through W. C. Fields, Laurel and Hardy, the Three Stooges, and the Marx Brothers. Don't neglect the screwball comedies of the thirties and forties (*Bringing Up Baby, His Girl Friday, My Man Godfrey*) and any of the Hope and Crosby "Road" pictures. Did you know that the comedies of Bob Hope were an early influence on Woody Allen?

Try to get a sense of what your genre of comedy might be. Romantic comedy (*How to Lose a Guy in 10 Days*), dark comedy (*Bad Santa*), fish-out-of-water teen comedy (*Mean Girls*), parody (*This Is Spinal Tap*), goofball comedy (*Tommy Boy*), spoof (*Scary Movie*), or just plain comedy without a label (*The Santa Clause*).

The only way to do that is to watch lots of comedies and find the ones that you not only like the best but relate to, also. The kind that makes you say: "I wish I wrote that!"

Are you *Ace Ventura: Pet Detective, Airplane, American Pie, Analyze This, Animal House, Barbershop, Being John Malkovich, Blazing Saddles, Fargo, Groundhog Day, Happy Gilmore, Heathers, Kingpin, Lost in Translation, Mean Girls, My Big Fat Greek Wedding, Porky's, Scary Movie, Shrek, Sideways, Splash, The Girl Next Door, The Graduate, Tootsie,* or *When Harry Met Sally*?

Are you Billy Wilder at his best: *Some Like It Hot, The Apartment*? Are you early Woody Allen, middle Woody Allen, or late Woody Allen? I love the guy, but if you study his work from *Take the Money and Run,* to *Annie Hall,* to *Zelig,* to *Crimes and Misdemeanors,* to *Deconstructing Harry,* to *Anything Else* you'll see the gamut of good, bad, brilliant, masterpiece, and just plain awful.

You probably have your own favorites. Watch them again, but this time study and analyze them. You probably have comedies you hate or laugh at *because* they're so bad. Watch them, too. It's easier to see the flaws in them.

You should also *read* as many comedy screenplays (as well as screenplays of all genres) as you can get your hands on. And I don't mean the published versions.

Find Web sites that let you buy scripts or download them for free. (Two of my favorites are www.script-o-rama.com and www.simply scripts.com. To find others type in "free screenplays" in your browser. You'll be surprised at what's available.) Sometimes you'll get first or second drafts. Occasionally, you'll find rejected drafts. If you don't want to print them out, read them off the screen. To me, the value of reading screenplays—of holding them in your hands—is that you get a stronger sense of the writers' intentions.

Reading interviews with comedy writers is also advantageous (again, as are interviews with screenwriters in general). Of even greater benefit is to read interviews with screenwriters whose work you admire. Hearing successful comedy writers talk about how they do it, where their ideas come from, tricks they've learned along the way, mistakes they've made, and pitfalls to avoid will make your entrée into comedy screenwriting less painful.

Get started. Make sure the first three pages are hilarious, so an agent or producer will keep reading. Remember to keep those laughs coming, but not at the expense of the story. The comedies we remember have memorable plots, extraordinary lines, and unforgettable moments.

Go ahead. Take your shot. Be funny.

May the laughs be with you.

# Finding Your Voice: Drama

Until lions have their historians,
tales of the hunt shall glorify the hunters.
−AFRICAN PROVERB

Back in Greece twenty-four hundred years ago, there was tragedy. Comedy was perceived to be a lesser form of writing because it was less serious. It still is today. Serious writers win Pulitzer Prizes, National Book Awards, and Tonys. Comedy writers win Emmys (occasionally Golden Globes and Oscars) and make tons of money.

Let's talk about tragedy.

According to our friend Aristotle (and you should come to think of him as your friend) this is the definition of tragedy:

*Tragedy, then, is an imitation of an action that is serious, complete and of a certain magnitude; in language embellished with each kind of artistic ornament, the several kinds being found in separate parts of the play; in the form of action, not of narrative; through pity and fear effecting the proper purgation of these emotions.*

Let's try a simpler definition:

*Tragedy is a composition, in prose or poetry, accommodated
to action and intended to exhibit a picture of human life or to
depict a series of grave or humorous actions of more than ordinary interest, tending toward some striking result. It is com-
monly designed to be spoken and represented by actors on
the stage.*

Here's an even simpler one:

*Tragedy is a drama or literary work in which the main character
is brought to ruin or suffers extreme sorrow, especially as a
consequence of a tragic flaw, moral weakness, or inability to
cope with unfavorable circumstances.*

Each definition pretty much says the same thing. Now let's go
back to Aristotle. Further reading of him exposes you to his thoughts
on Fear and Pity.

Fear and Pity are at the core of drama.

I'll simplify it.

Tragedy (drama) must inspire Fear and Pity in an audience.

- I'm glad that's not me.
- Thank God that didn't happen to me.
- After seeing what happened to *him,* I'll never do *that* again.
- If that can happen to *her,* it can happen to *me.*

**Recommended:** Aristotle's *Poetics* translated by S. H. Butcher,
with an introductory essay by Francis Fergusson. There are numerous translations, but in my opinion this is the best.

Have you ever read a story in the newspaper or heard about something that happened to someone you know that shook you up?

I live in New York City. I do a lot of walking. I always seem to be in a hurry. Even when I'm not going anywhere in particular I walk fast and I'm impatient. When I'm crossing the street, instead of being a responsible pedestrian and waiting on the curb for the light so I can cross, I take a few steps into the street. This is stupid and dangerous, because Manhattan is filled with inconsiderate bike riders and reckless drivers.

On several occasions I've almost been hit by cars making a turn after the light changed or bicyclists ignoring a red light.

I once stood in the street, several steps off of the curb, being my impatient self. There was another guy even more impatient. He was about three feet in front of me, anxious to get across the street. We both were looking to our right, watching the oncoming traffic, waiting for it to subside so we could cross. The cars slowed. The light was about to change.

Suddenly, out of nowhere, a kid on a bike who'd been part of the traffic ignored the changing red light and kept coming.

I saw him and stepped back. The guy in front of me didn't see him. The kid plowed into the guy, sending him to the ground. He was traumatized. His body was shaking. Somebody nearby called 911.

My first reactions to what I saw were as follows:

- That could've been me.
- Thank God it wasn't me.
- I'll never move off the curb again.
- That poor guy. I wonder if he'll be okay?

The best movies that are considered dramas or serious or "not comedies" deal with a lead character who suffers an almost intolerable crisis (*A Beautiful Mind, Far from Heaven, The Insider, The Fisher King, Forrest Gump,* to name a few).

There are other films that certainly aren't comedies but are definitely dramas or melodramas in which the lead character undergoes some sort of crisis or challenge, but not one as difficult as the aforementioned films (*Searching for Bobby Fisher, The Verdict, Finding Neverland, Million Dollar Baby*).

If you're going to write "serious" films, make sure that the problem your main character has is big enough to result in an emotional connection with your audience.

To this day stories about the Holocaust still resonate.

Newspaper headlines are filled almost daily with tragic events overflowing with drama. As I write this the biggest story in the country is that of Terri Schiavo, the brain-damaged woman in Florida whose family fought to the highest court in the land to let her live. Why were people drawn to her tragic plight? Because of its inherent life-and-death struggle.

Drama is everywhere in life. Any person not adjusted to his environment suggests drama. As the saying goes, "Shit happens." Legendary acting teacher Stella Adler said it nicer: "Life intrudes."

There was a book a while back called *When Bad Things Happen to Good People*. The title says it all. Bad things *do* happen to good people and within a good person's crisis there is drama and because you're a screenwriter it's up to you to find the story.

## Lecture 18

# Are You Cheap or Deep?

Many a man has finally succeeded only because he has
failed after repeated efforts. If he had never met
defeat he would never have known any great victory.
—ORISON SWETT MARDEN

Do you substitute cheap emotion for deep emotion? If you're writing
dumb comedies instead of scripts with intelligence and wit, you might
be perceived as a hack. You might make a lot of money writing stupid
stuff, but you may not get much respect.

That's not to say that you can't write an incredibly commercial
script that's also got some depth.

Depth scares most of Hollywood.

I think that in most cases the studios are afraid that audiences are
intimidated by depth. So screenwriters are backed into a horrible cor-
ner where they have to dumb down their clever stories with the un-
predictable twists and turns. If they don't, some other writer will be
hired to do it for them. And that writer will probably make it worse. So
the original writer does what he's told and his inspired script becomes hackneyed and trite.

I think you should aim for the deep emotion and hope it gets
through, rather than going for the cheap stuff first time around.

It'll be more fun for you and you'll keep your self-respect. On the other hand, sometimes a script borders on being cheap when all it really needs is to be smarter.

## Does Your Script Need an Injection of Smart?

How "smart" a script is could mean the difference between a sale and a "No thanks."

What does "smart" mean?

A producer I know uses the word a lot. He uses the word to describe the last pass he (and the writer he's working with) takes on a screenplay before sending it out to the studios, stars, or directors.

What this producer means is this: There are no scenes that go on a sentence too long or stage directions that are too verbose. There are no plot points that seemed so cool but are too cool or not cool enough. There are no lines that are a little too precious. If the screenplay's a comedy, the lines are worthy of a feature film and not too sit-comy.

I think it's smart (and professional) to give your script an injection of smart by making one final pass before sending it out. You may only find yourself adjusting a few lines here and there, but it'll definitely make the script better.

Another way to make your screenplay deeper and smarter is to channel your frustration into the script.

## Use Anger to Fuel Your Screenplay

Let's say you spent nearly two years perfecting your new screenplay only to find that on the day you were gonna take it to the photocopy shop to make copies to send out, trade publications such as *Variety* or *The Hollywood Reporter* announced the sale or greenlighting of a project just like yours.

You're screwed.

Your script is dead in the water. At least for a while. It may be for a few years. Maybe forever.

You have to hope that there will come a time when studios and producers are looking for what you wrote. At which time you'll pull it out and send it out all over again. Screenwriters usually find out what industry people are looking for through agents, managers, and producers with inside contacts.

I know lots of writers, including myself, who either were almost done with a script, had just finished it, were just getting it out there, or were getting good vibes from an agent or producer only to be blown out of the water by the news that a similar screenplay was on its way to the screen.

Your first reaction is rage coupled with the concern that somebody stole your idea. Then you might get down on yourself for not finishing the thing sooner or being more aggressive in getting it out there.

At the end of the day, once you've calmed down and realized there's nothing you can do about this project, you can try to utilize that anger to fuel your next project.

Professionals keep going. Whiners, complainers, and babies feed on their misery and end up defeating themselves by not going back to the computer and starting again.

I know that some people, maybe the majority of people, aren't resilient enough to dust themselves off and get back on the horse that threw them. But it's the screenwriter who "keeps on keepin' on," as Satchel Paige once said, that will reap the reward.

## Who Is Your Energy?

Until you have an agent or manager you're fighting the good fight alone. If you have an agent or manager or both it doesn't necessarily mean that they're doing anything for you. If you're suddenly hot, then they'll make phone calls all over town. But because you're hot they won't need to. Producers, studios, and networks will be calling you.

In my own experience with agents, as well as that of my friends, colleagues, and former students, if agents aren't pushing you they're pushing someone else. They *will* push you if you give them a kick-ass new script that's got a cool, high-concept premise that's highly commercial, but how often do you give them one of those? If you do, you have to hope that something just like it didn't sell the week before, because then your agent won't return your calls.

This isn't about agents. It's about the person providing the energy for your career. Until you become hot or at least get a little heat the only person who'll be there for you is, well, *you.*

This means that not only are you the soldier fighting the good fight in the field, but you're also the general directing the war effort.

It means doing your homework. Read the trade publications. Subscribe if you have the money. If not, most libraries stock *Variety.* Check out the numerous Internet screenwriting sites. I recommend www. scriptsales.com and http://hollywoodlitsales.com for starters. There are several magazines devoted entirely to screenwriting. (See Resources section.)

Besides writing your screenplays, you have to make the calls to agents, managers, and producers, write the letters, send the e-mails, do the networking and schmoozing. It means being relentless and maybe a little pushy (or a lot if you have that mechanism). Being nice and warm and fuzzy never seems to work. Politeness goes only so far. What I've found is that appearing to be confident (even if you're cowering inside) tends to work.

If you're naturally confident, tough, aggressive, don't care if people like you, and are not worried about your mother being disappointed in you for not being nice—wait a minute . . . if you're like this you should be an agent, not a screenwriter.

Look, here's the deal: Be your own energy. Nobody else gives a damn. Even when you get representation, be your own energy.

# Now!

## Lecture 19

# Diving Headfirst into Your
# Full-Length Screenplay

A deadline is negative inspiration.
Still, it's better than no inspiration at all.
—RITA MAE BROWN

By now you should have your outline, three-act story line, or treatment. You're ready to start writing the script.

In my screenwriting classes students usually spend two to three weeks working on their outlines and the rest of the semester writing their screenplays. That breaks down to ten or eleven weeks.

I suggest you give yourself at least ten weeks to do your first draft. Shoot for ten to fifteen pages a week.

Some weeks you'll get more, some weeks less.

Because you're working on your own, you'll have to create your own discipline. Pretend that every Monday morning you have to turn in ten to fifteen pages for me to read. That might help. I'm suggesting Monday so you'll have the weekend to work on the script in the event your schedule during the week is hectic.

You know about plotting, characterization, dialogue, structure, and act breaks.

There's nothing else to do except to start writing.

Once you finish your first draft refer to Lecture 6. Everything I said about rewriting a short screenplay is applicable to rewriting a full-length one.

## Screenplay Format
## (In case you don't know)

Final Draft (or any screenwriting program) will do the formatting for you, but you should know the basics.

**EXAMPLE #1**

FADE IN ON

A shelf filled with books featuring famous fictional detectives: Philip Marlowe, Mike Hammer, Hercule Poirot, and so on.

And on a shelf all their own, novels featur-
ing famous <u>African-American detectives</u>: John
Shaft, Easy Rawlins, Blanche White, Coffin Ed
Johnson, Alex Cross, and so on.

PULLBACK REVEALS that we're in the bedroom
of WESLEY COBB, 29, African-American. Trim,
cool. He's at his desk staring at a list of
names on his PowerBook. Nelly plays in the
background.

                    REX THRASHER
                    THOR CUMMINGS
                    YANCY BURDETTE
                    NICK CONTESSA

BUCK HALSTEAD
LUKE MONTANA

Using the hunt-and-peck method, Wesley types
in another name: ULYSSES POTTS. Leans back.
Smiles.

LEONARD COBB, Wesley's father, 68, enters
the room.

                    WESLEY
  Hey, Pop! Whattya think of Ulysses Potts?

                    LEONARD
  Sounds like a pro basketball player,
  not a private detective.
                  (beat)
  Let's go. You don't want to be late
  for your first class.

                    WESLEY
  How 'bout Ichabod Smythe?

                    LEONARD
  Way too gay. Besides, ain't no black man
  *ever* named Ichabod.

Wesley nods in agreement. Stands up. Reaches
for a CANE. He moves slowly out of the room.

CAM PANS to the dresser, where we see a gun
in a holster.

**EXAMPLE #2**

INT. WESLEY COBB'S BEDROOM—DAY

CLOSE ON A shelf filled with books featuring famous fictional detectives: Philip Marlowe, Mike Hammer, Hercule Poirot, and so on.

And on a shelf all their own, novels featuring famous <u>African-American detectives</u>: John Shaft, Easy Rawlins, Blanche White, Coffin Ed Johnson, Alex Cross, and so on.

WESLEY COBB, 29, African-American. Trim, cool. He's at his desk staring at a list of names on his Powerbook. Nelly plays in the background.

> REX THRASHER
> THOR CUMMINGS
> YANCY BURDETTE
> NICK CONTESSA
> BUCK HALSTEAD
> LUKE MONTANA

Using the hunt-and-peck method, Wesley types in another name: ULYSSES POTTS. Leans back. Smiles.

LEONARD COBB, Wesley's father, 68, enters the room.

                    WESLEY
Hey, Pop! Whattya think of Ulysses Potts?


                    LEONARD
Sounds like a pro basketball player,
not a private detective.
                    (beat)
Let's go. You don't want to be late
for your first class.


                    WESLEY
How 'bout Ichabod Smythe?


                    LEONARD
Way too gay. Besides, ain't no black man
<u>ever</u> named Ichabod.


Wesley nods in agreement. Stands up. Reaches
for a CANE. He moves slowly out of the room.


CAM PANS to the dresser, where we see a gun
in a holster.


The only difference between these two pages is the Fade In shot.

Most screenplays begin like Example #2, by having a Slug Line
that defines the place and time.

However, some screenplays, for dramatic effect, begin like Example #1.

It's a matter of your own style. After you've written two or three
screenplays you'll know what you prefer.

# Part VI

# How to Be a Well-Rounded Writer, Director, and All-round Film Buff

Most people don't realize that writing is a craft. You have to take your apprenticeship in it like everything else.

–COLE PORTER

# Lecture 20

# Create Your Own Cinema Studies Department

Inspiration comes from working every day.
–CHARLES BAUDELAIRE

Being a filmmaker means that you love movies. It also means not only directing them but also watching them.

I won't say who he is, but I used to belong to the same video store as a famous A-list director. You would recognize the name instantly. He's been making movies for more than thirty years. He is a giant in the industry.

I saw him in the video store on numerous occasions, always checking out two or three films or browsing around. I once asked the clerk what kind of films the famous director checked out and he said all kinds.

I hate going to movies at night when there are crowds. To me, crowds mean people talking during the movie, which drives me crazy. So I often go to a movie on a Sunday morning, usually the first show, which is typically 10:30 A.M.

So one Sunday I'm sitting in one of the theaters in my local tenplex. I don't remember the movie, but I remember that I was the only one in the theater.

Then I see somebody else come in.

Guess who?

The same famous director.

At 10:30 on a Sunday morning.

This guy *loves* movies.

So do I.

So should you.

I'm not saying that you should cover every inch of your room or apartment with movie posters, although that would be fine. I'm simply saying that you should start immersing yourself in the past and present of the film business while keeping an eye on the future.

How do you go about becoming a film buff?

It's not that hard.

You can start by turning on your TV.

- Watch the Sundance Channel, the Independent Film Channel, American Movie Classics, and Turner Classic Movies. I don't mean just "watch" the movies. Study them. Think about them. Look at the way stories are told. Pay attention to the structure. The dialogue, the lighting, the camera angles. Observe everything on the screen with a keen eye.

- Start your own library of books on or about filmmaking. Read biographies and autobiographies of past and present directors, screenwriters, and producers. I've been reading and collecting books like these for twenty years. Here are a few of my favorites: *The Film Director as Superstar* by Joseph Gelmis, *Kazan: The Master Director Discusses His Films* by Jeff Young (editor), *Easy Riders, Raging Bulls: How the Sex-Drugs-and-Rock 'n' Roll Generation Saved Hollywood* by Peter Biskind, *The Mailroom: Hollywood History from the Bottom Up* by David Rensin, *The Studio* by John Gregory Dunne, *Hello, He Lied* by Lynda Obst, *The Kid Stays in the Picture* by Robert Evans, and *Elia Kazan: A Life* by Elia Kazan.

- Become knowledgeable about how the movie business started. Learn how the movie studios controlled every aspect of their productions, in what was sometimes referred to as the "studio system." There are wonderful biographies of the early moguls such as Darryl F. Zanuck, Samuel Goldwyn, Irving Thalberg, Louis B. Mayer, and David O. Selznick, to mention a few. Again, my personal library is filled with two dozen books on these gentlemen and their era. Here are a few recommendations: *A Memo from David O. Selznick* by David Selznick, *Twentieth Century's Fox: Darryl F. Zanuck and the Culture of Hollywood* by George F. Custen, *Hollywood East: Louis B. Mayer and the Origins of the Studio System* by Diana Altman, *Goldwyn: A Biography* by A. Scott Berg, and *My Autobiography* by Charles Chaplin.

- Study films from the masters of other countries. Akira Kurosawa, Federico Fellini, Michelangelo Antonioni, Lina Wertmuller, David Lean, Bernardo Bertolucci, Ingmar Bergman, Jean-Luc Godard, François Truffaut, Rainer Werner Fassbinder, Werner Herzog (to name a few).

- Check out the ever-growing number of Internet sites devoted to movies. (See Resources section.)

- You may be doing this already, but if not, rent or buy DVDs and check out the commentaries. Many DVDs have interviews with directors and screenwriters along with detailed information on how certain scenes were storyboarded and shot. These extra features offer incredible information on making movies. The DVDs of Robert Rodriguez's films are extremely valuable, regardless of whether you actually like his movies or not. Definitely check out *El Mariachi,* his first feature. He talks about the cheap but effective methods he used to light the film and record the sound. You'll find it quite inspiring.

If you're going to write screenplays and make films, you owe it to yourself to become as informed and knowledgeable about the industry and the great talents who've left their marks in it.

You can be a screenwriter and you can be a director. Why not also add "film historian" to your résumé?

# Lecture 21

# The Importance of a Good Read

Writing done too quickly always
has to be done again.
–ROBERTSON DAVIES

I think the expression "a good read" started in the world of publishing. It refers to a book that's an entertaining, pleasurable reading experience.

Screenplays should be like that, too.

A film producer friend told me he gravitates to scripts that leap off the page. When he first said those words I was new to screenwriting and I didn't completely understand what he meant. It wasn't until I started reading lots of screenplays that I got it.

To me, a script that leaps off the page is fun to read no matter what the genre. Not only is the dialogue compelling, but so are the stage directions.

What was a fun screenplay? Two by Shane Black: *The Last Boy Scout* and *The Long Kiss Goodnight. Die Hard* by Steven DeSouza. Quentin Tarantino's stuff is fun, especially *Kill Bill*–all 201 pages of it. (That's right. 201. It breaks all the rules of polite screenwriting society. And it works. But that's another story.) *Exit Zero* by Kurt Wimmer was a blast to read. These all happen to be action scripts, but David Mamet's *Glengarry Glen Ross* wasn't. He adapted his talky two-set hour-long play into one of the most fun (and best) scripts I've had the pleasure of reading. *Home Alone* by John Hughes wasn't an action movie. Neither was Emma Thompson's screen version of *Sense and Sensibility.* Paul Rudnick's *In and Out* was a laugh riot from page 1.

I could name a few more. Some have been made; some are in pre-production or development. Some have been written by former students and friends of mine.

The key word being "few." I have to believe that if I were an agent or producer I would love to find a screenplay that isn't so much as a business decision but ninety minutes of pleasure.

It ought to be fun.

Put yourself in the place of someone whose job it is to find screen-plays to represent, produce, or convince studios to finance. To that in-dividual, reading scripts is indeed a "job." And if most of the screenplays are bad or so-so or derivative it is a job that becomes boring, frustrating, and maddening.

So when a screenplay arrives that hooks someone from the first scene or by the bottom of the first page, she's going to relax. If each page makes her laugh or gets her emotionally invested in the story and if that enjoyment is sustained to the last page, that person is ex-periencing a fun read.

Readers and story analysts—people who literally make their living reading scripts—appreciate a fun read more than anyone. When you spend your days, weeks, and even years reading screenplays it's easy to become jaded. I've known several professional readers, and to a person, they'll tell you that they can barely get through most of what they read. But when that one script that does indeed jump off the page and entertain and maybe even enthrall comes along, these people are in heaven.

Often word will spread throughout Hollywood about a hot spec script that's making the rounds.

It's so good that everybody who reads it loves it. It develops a buzz and the buzz sometimes turns into a bidding frenzy where studios, producers, directors, and stars are drooling to get involved with the project.

Trust me: The buzz started because the script was a fun read.

How do you make your script fun to read? There's no easy answer. Maybe only a few guidelines. I bet you can guess what I'm going to say. A compelling, believable story helps. An interesting main character who's likable and flawed and who we want to root for. Dialogue that is crisp, fresh, and spare. Stage directions that don't overwhelm. Plot twists and turns that keep us guessing and surprised and anticipating what will be happening next. And as we turn the last few pages a wonderfully satisfying ending. One more thing: that after we read "The End" we find ourselves wishing it hadn't ended.

# Lecture 22

# More Stuff You Should Know
# About Writing

I put a piece of paper under my pillow,
and when I could not sleep I wrote in the dark.
–HENRY DAVID THOREAU

## Conflict

Two people getting along is boring to read (and watch). It's not that you have to write scenes in which two or more people are yelling and screaming at each other. That would be easy. What's hard is to write the subtle kind of conflict that shows how people are headed for trouble.

More writers than you would imagine have trouble in this area.

For a very brief time I went out with a woman who, unbeknownst to me, was, for lack of a better description, a party animal. Her idea of fun was going *out* around 10 or 11:00 P.M. and barhopping, drinking, and dancing until 3:00 A.M. I was, well, different. I preferred to get *in* by 10:00 or 11:00 P.M. after a movie or play or dinner. I only drank *with* dinner, and dancing was something I only did at weddings.

One of us had to change if we were going to go anywhere as a couple. She was bored with my idea of fun and I didn't have the constitution to do what she enjoyed. We each tried to adapt, but it didn't work.

It couldn't work.

There were no screaming arguments. The "conflict" was all subtext. I'd be miserable out with her in a club and she'd be miserable heading back home from a Broadway play at 10:30.

So the relationship ended (not that it ever got to a serious stage) and we were both happier, not to mention better off.

However, the conflict that transpired between us was monumental. Only it was understated. It made us both uncomfortable. Her friends probably heard her complaining about how dull I was, just as my friends heard me complaining how I couldn't keep up with her.

It would've been very entertaining if it were written in a script.

Bottom line: If you're having trouble putting your characters in situations that make them uncomfortable, put them with someone who loves everything they hate.

## The Character Arc

Call it what you will: character arc or the journey the character takes. In even the worst movie ever made the main character should undergo a change, presumably for the better. In real life people tend not to change. We continue making the same mistakes over and over again. But in art, presumably, there is change in varying degrees. Scrooge comes to mind as the character in literature who changed the most drastically, but even a small change is good, too.

The problem is not deciding "how" a character changes but what he changes from. Is he a bad guy or a guy who's rough around the edges or just insensitive? Is he a raging drunk, functioning alcoholic, or steady drinker? Is he a weakling or a coward or a heel?

The thing we all have to do is pinpoint our character's flaws and weaknesses, then incorporate them into his persona in such a way as to make someone reading the script recognize that this is a flesh-and-blood, recognizable human being.

Actors love playing complicated, complex, troubled characters. I can't tell you how many times I've heard actors (major stars) say they love playing bad guys. Just look at Al Pacino's movies. You won't see too many easygoing guys there without a care in the world.

People have problems.

And secrets.

And things they've done that they're ashamed of.

People without a conscience can get through the night. People with a conscience and a sense of guilt and regret or shame have a rough go of it.

Characters who behave badly in whatever degree or whichever way need to go through a journey that makes them change. If the change doesn't happen on-screen by the end of the film the audience should have a sense that the beginning of change is at hand.

Make sure you give your main characters a good starting point on their way to becoming different, better people.

## Sex Scenes

Unless you're writing something like *Boogie Nights,* where sex scenes are integral to the story, be careful. In an era when porn (both hard-core and soft) can be seen on TV or the Internet, sex scenes in mainstream movies may only accomplish one thing: slowing down the dramatic tension of the plot.

In the past, say starting with *Easy Rider* and *Midnight Cowboy* in the late sixties, where sex scenes were actually nude scenes, there would be a snippet of flesh or naked bodies writhing and that would be it. Jon Voight and Sylvia Miles rolling around on her bed was pretty shocking in 1969.

Other films of the seventies and eighties pushed the envelope even further by having major female stars bare breasts and butts and do "nude" scenes. For most moviegoers of that era it was probably titillating to see movie stars naked or seminaked, especially if the scene was erotically directed and acted.

Now, my guess is a large percentage of the moviegoing audience (especially males) is desensitized to sex scenes or nude scenes because of the aforementioned easy access to porn in our own living rooms. Women might find the scenes tedious unless they're romantic or tastefully done. There are those who might argue that a sex scene is crucial to some stories in order to heighten a dramatic moment or illustrate a point, i.e., *Monster's Ball*. Did we really need to *see* the graphic scene between Halle Berry and Billy Bob Thornton? Or would the implication that they were going to have sex have been enough? Who knows? The filmmakers made a choice. Would the film have been any less compelling if we didn't watch the two characters having sex? In my opinion, no.

Same with *Sideways*. There was a fairly graphic scene in which a character had to sneak into a bedroom while a couple was having sex. Was it erotic? Hardly. It was hilarious and a highly dramatic moment in the film. Did the filmmakers have to have the couple in bed naked rather than, say, in their kitchen fully clothed, eating dinner? Well it wouldn't have been as dangerous or humorous. This was an instance where a sex scene lent itself perfectly to the movie.

Sooooo . . . if you're determined to have your two lead characters participate in a steamy sex scene (or if the people financing your movie insist upon it), do it. Or if you have an idea for a scene of a sexual nature that might get you a laugh or heighten a dramatic moment, go for it.

Ideally, stay away from gratuitous sex scenes. Most of the time they're laughable when you read them.

## Suspension of Disbelief

It's the ability of a story to encourage its audience to suspend their disbelief and go along with events as they unfold.

Stories don't have to be real, but they must appear to be real, at least for the duration of the movie. Spiderman *can* fly. Jedi knights *do* control the minds of others through the force. Marty McFly (Michael J. Fox in *Back to the Future*) really did travel back in time in a turbo-charged DeLorean.

If you give your audience the appearance of truth they'll follow you anywhere. It's when you try to pull a fast one on your audience that you get in trouble. *Kate & Leopold,* released in 2001, comes to mind. The plot is basically this: A guy living in the present finds a space near the Brooklyn Bridge where there is a gap in time. He goes back to the nineteenth century and takes pictures of the place. Leopold, a man living in the 1870s, puzzled by Stuart's tiny camera, decides to follow him and they both end up in the twenty-first century.

The movie was actually not bad if you viewed it as a love story. (Leopold meets Meg Ryan in the present.) But the entire foundation of the script fell apart because the filmmakers didn't do a believable, *truthful* job of convincing the audience of how the original guy traveled back in time and how Leopold got back to the present with him.

All I could think of throughout the movie was that I didn't believe Leopold *really* traveled in time. However, I had no problem believing that Michael J. Fox did in *Back to the Future.*

## Why Second and Third Acts Are So Hard

In Act One you've introduced the world of your main character, had the Instigating Event happen, and introduced the Major Dramatic Question. You're moving along nicely to the end of Act One. You're feeling good and confident and secretly thinking you'll finish this one in a couple of weeks.

Then you find yourself stuck in Act Two. Here's something to ease the pain.

Make sure that dramatic complications arise from the situation you have set up in Act One. While it sounds pretty simple and basic, this is where most screenwriters go off track. They haven't come up with enough complications and obstacles to get in the way of the protagonist. Or the ones they did come up with weren't very difficult.

Look at it like this: Make life miserable for your main character. We need to feel sorry for him/her in order for us to root for him/her. (Since I'm tired of saying "him/her" I'll just say "him.") Make everything in his path not go his way. He has to actively get past each obstacle. Some can be easy, but the further into the script you go, the more and more difficult they should become, with the most difficult coming near the end.

It sounds pretty simple, right?

In reality it's very hard to do.

A cool example of this is *Clean and Sober,* a fine film written by Tod Carroll, directed by Glenn Gordon Caron, and starring Michael Keaton. We meet the protagonist early one morning. He's a hotshot real estate agent in bed with a naked woman. He's awake. He thinks she's asleep. We quickly learn that they've been on a cocaine binge. He tries to wake her, only to discover that her body is ice cold. She's dead. The police come. He's a suspect. He's told not to leave town. Of course, he tries to leave town. But at the airport his credit card is refused. And he doesn't have cash. We also learn that besides having a coke problem, he's an alcoholic.

He gets the idea that he can hide out from the cops for a while by checking into a rehab facility. He does so, but it's a big joke to him. He tries to score drugs while there. He hits on women while there. After a brief period he's told to leave.

Simultaneously, we've learned that he has stolen nearly one hundred thousand dollars of a client's money for personal use. He must replace it or face dire repercussions. So on top of dealing with his booze and drug problems and the dead girl in his bed, he has this major career/money problem.

He tries to get people to lend him money. He fails. Finally, he decides that going into rehab might not be a bad idea. That decision brings us to the end of Act One.

So a lot of stuff happened to him. As we get into Acts Two and Three more stuff happens to him as he gradually starts to take the program seriously. He makes enemies. He falls for a woman. He goes through the hell of drug withdrawal. Without spoiling the movie for you, suffice it to say that as the character gets further and further into the world of drug and alcohol rehabilitation, things get worse for him before they get better.

Definitely rent it.

## Binge Writing

Some people can't sit at their computers and consider it a good writing day if they turn out three pages. They have to grind out forty or their self-esteem plunges into the gutter. This is binge writing. It has both good and bad points. The good part is that at least you have a bunch of pages from which to build. The bad part is that most of the binge writers I've encountered have blown their wad. They exhausted themselves churning out the forty pages to such an extent that they've lost their passion for the story.

They might be able to go forward and do another forty pages, but they tend to resist doing revisions on the first forty. They've simply lost interest to such an extent that they'd rather start a new idea and grind out another forty pages only to find themselves bored with *that* material.

Binge writing might work for some, provided they have the ability to revise and rewrite. As for me, I'll happily take three pages every day that I can maintain my enthusiasm for so much so that I can either keep the story moving or happily revise what I've got. So write, but don't go overboard just so you can count up pages.

## How to Deal with Writer's Block

If I had the solution for writer's block I'd be a happy man. I've had it for the last month. The day begins with me having the best of intentions to get cracking at that third act that's been stumping me. Then that day turns into two, then three, then a week, then two weeks, then a month. By this point the self-loathing starts to kick in.

I like self-loathing. It's the way I feel after I've binged on a pint of Ben and Jerry's Cherry Garcia. It's only after the self-loathing that I feel ready to start dieting and, well, writing.

I have a body of work to my credit: four published plays that are still being produced, three pilot deals, episodes on a few sitcoms, two sold screenplays that haven't been made (yet), treatments optioned plus other plays that had productions or workshops, three published books, and a slew of other screenplays that nothing happened to.

Mainly, I look at the stack of stuff I've done and, if I'm to be honest, I'd have to say that some are just okay, some are pretty bad, a few are pretty good, and maybe three things are *really* good, so that I'm proud of them.

But on each and every project, whether good or bad, I had writer's block. Somehow I got through it and finished each project. I've started other screenplays, as well as treatments, television projects, and plays, and not completed them, but I've never given up on something that had more than fifty pages. I've always figured that if I hit page 50 I could keep going and achieve the balance.

I have lots of false starts. Ten pages here, twenty pages there. Sometimes a first act. Either I lost interest or couldn't make it work or found out that it was similar to a movie that was just released in theaters or I heard about a sale, so I abandoned it.

Other circumstances may lead to you giving up on a script, but writer's block doesn't have to be one of them.

Writer's block is like a batting slump for a baseball player. He can take batting practice every day. He can concentrate or indulge in his favorite rituals and superstitions. He can be more careful and patient when he's at bat. But if he's missing the ball or his timing's off and he's only getting a small piece of the ball and if he's hitting it hard but right to a fielder . . . he's just not gonna get a hit.

He's in a slump. He can keep playing and hoping. But deep down he knows he has to wait it out. Just like a writer has to wait out *his* slump.

The point is that writer's blocks eventually end.

Some last longer than others. But if you're patient, trust me, it will end.

Until the next one comes.

## Setting Time Limits

I've talked to enough screenwriters about the process of writing and completing a screenplay to know that everyone approaches it differently.

If you're working on a paying job, your motivation is to not waste time or take too long to turn in a draft so you won't be fired. Money certainly has a way of pushing even the laziest of writers.

It's different when you're doing something on spec or if you're in school or you have a day job or are married and have responsibilities to your spouse or if you have a kid or more than one kid. Suddenly, finding the *time* to write becomes a huge priority.

Unless you have incredible discipline and are able to set aside an hour or more a day no matter how busy you are, finding the time to write is a challenge.

What has worked for many of the screenwriters I know is to wait until a chunk of time becomes available. Say you're a student and you have winter or spring break. Or the summer. If you're out of school you may have a week or two vacation. Or the busy season has ended in your profession.

What you want to look for is a window of opportunity to finish that script that's been nagging away at you.

A screenwriter I know found himself with a chunk of time, roughly two months, when he was free to work on whatever he pleased for most of the day. He decided to return to a script that he'd started four years earlier. He'd worked on it sporadically, between assignments and between a book that he'd managed to write. He'd completed two-thirds of the script, had a vague idea of where the second act would end and an even more vague idea of what the third act would be.

He had no other irons in the fire and, after reading the pages he'd written, decided that he would devote those two months to completing the script. All the usual distractions came, including a handful of new ideas that sounded vastly more fun to start than concentrating on nailing down a workable third act on his four-year project.

He lost momentum. Got it back, then lost it again and was ready to throw in the towel. He found himself in that horrible position of hating the idea and everything he'd written.

Guess what? He finished a draft. Not in the two months he allotted himself but in seven weeks. Then he passed it around to his circle of critics, or Dutch uncles, if you will, and he got their respective notes and spent another two weeks rewriting and revising the script.

What he's enjoying telling people is that if he hadn't set his mind to finishing the script in those two months, he knows he wouldn't have done it. The script would still be one of many unfinished documents in his screenplay file.

Carving out time has worked for me. It worked for him. Maybe it can work for you.

**Colloquium**

# How to Avoid Getting Screwed in Hollywood

Creativity is a continual surprise.

–RAY BRADBURY

Once you've written (revised and done three or four rewrites on) a full-length screenplay you're ready to take things to the next level.

You have to get an agent or manager (or both) who will try to sell your script to (or use it as a writing sample for) producers and studio executives.

There's no right or easy way of getting an agent or manager. Referrals are the best way: from friends, teachers, family, producers who've read and liked your script. If you don't have anyone to refer you (and most new screenwriters don't), it means you have to dig in your heels and be aggressive.

This means finding the names of agents and managers who are willing to read unsolicited material. Checking out the many screenwriting Web sites and screenwriting magazines is the best way to start.

While you're busy trying to find an agent or manager, you should also pursue producers. You have to send out your script yourself to production companies. Where do you find production companies? It's not as difficult as you might think. Check out the Hollywood Cre-

Whether you're sending your script to producers yourself or you've managed to get an agent, the next best thing to selling a script is having someone important like it. Not enough to buy it or produce it but enough to take a meeting with you to discuss other ideas or to indicate an interest in reading your next script.

ative Directory. Go to their Web site: www.hcdonline.com. The Writers Guild of America has another good site.

Most production companies are in Los Angeles; some are in New York. Major actors and directors have production companies. You have nothing to lose by sending your script to them, as long as you have the name of someone at the company. Producers have staffs filled with anywhere from two people to more than a dozen. Some of the employees are Development Executives. Their job is to read scripts that presumably the producer would be interested in producing. Studios have Development Executives, too.

Over the years, Development Executives have gotten the nicknames D-boys and D-girls. They can become your best friend or your worst nightmare.

Many D-boys and D-girls are producers and screenwriters themselves. It's actually a cool job for someone out of college and interested in breaking into the film business. You get a crash course in how projects are chosen, how the system works. Depending on the size of a company, there can be anywhere from one D-boy or D-girl to five or six. They answer to the director of development, who answers to the president of the company.

In larger production companies there is a hierarchy of Development Executives starting at the entry level. At the bottom of the barrel are college interns, typically followed by former interns hired full-time upon graduation, the young relative of one of the principals, or an aggressive film buff who wrote a kick-ass letter that got her in the door.

The interns and former interns most likely will read unsolicited screenplays generally assumed to be awful or scripts recommended by people on the periphery of the film industry, i.e., people who haven't produced a film but want to.

These entry-level readers aspire to the next level, which means reading scripts that are presumably better because they've been formally submitted by lesser (or new) agents and managers. The presumption here is that they don't necessarily have the best writers as clients.

The next rung on the development ladder is probably the best spot, because they get to read scripts submitted by the best agents and managers (presumed to be representing the best writers).

A development person at any level submits his reports to the director of development. This person probably has a nice office but not a lot of power other than access to the person or people who can say yes to a script.

Depending on the muscle of an agent or manager, some scripts are submitted straight to the director of development for a read. Fortunate is the screenwriter whose script has bypassed the underlings. It means you've circumvented a potential stumbling block. Avoiding lots of stumbling blocks is how screenplays get sold (and made).

Even luckier is the screenwriter whose agent or manager has a personal relationship with the top dog of a company. In these instances even the director of development is bypassed and the script is sent directly to the person in charge.

## Why the Person in Charge Can Change Your Life

When the big shot likes your script you're in, because no matter how good or bad it is, if the person in charge likes it, it suddenly becomes a "Project in Development," meaning that your screenplay is being seriously considered as a film that will get made.

Jumping to the head of the line isn't the norm. What's typical is the slow progression of a screenplay through a string of development people at a string of production companies until somebody likes it enough to recommend it to the director of development, who reads it and likes it and recommends it to the boss, who also likes it but who typically will feel that it needs work.

This is where the story takes a, well, unique turn.

If a D-boy you're working with has a deep understanding, knowledge, and love of films and film history and, say, a degree in Cinema Studies from a first-rate film school (rather than an MBA from Wharton or Stanford), he could very well be your knight in shining armor. He will read your script and call you in for a meeting during which he'll point out what works, what doesn't work, why it doesn't work, and (if you're really lucky) what you might do to fix it.

After talking to him you will feel pumped and confident and actually look forward to starting the next draft because, after all, you know what the development person wants. He gave you some constructive feedback that you can use. Maybe he handed you several pages of written notes or gave you back your script with comments and suggestions throughout. To complete the picture, throughout the meeting there was serious schmoozing and laughs and chitchat about topics other than the script.

Maybe he said the magic words: "We have another project that needs a rewrite and you're the one to do it."

As you walk out the door, you feel as if you're in love. Your pride hasn't been wounded and your dignity is intact.

Unfortunately, there is another kind of Development Executive who will take you on a different journey.

She's the type who got the job solely because somebody had a daughter who kind of liked movies and needed a job after getting out of rehab, so an old favor was called in. There's also the old school ties factor and the looks factor, especially with women. People with connections or a perceived pedigree get development positions even if their idea of a great film is *Breakin' 2: Electric Boogaloo*.

These are the D-boys and D-girls who give development a bad name. They might skim but not read your screenplay. Depending on their mood they may read only the dialogue or only the stage directions. They may get to the first ten pages, read a few in the middle of Act Two and maybe the last ten pages.

Their comments will be generalities like "It doesn't go far enough," "It doesn't raise the bar," "It isn't smart enough," and my favorite: "It's too predictable." (Duh, aren't most movies predictable? How many films have you seen in the last six months where you didn't know [or didn't have a pretty good idea] how they would turn out? Unless it's a really awful film, I don't mind knowing where it's going. As long as I'm entertained, I'm along for the ride. As a great thinker once said, "It's the journey, not the destination.")

The irony is that once a script has gone through the wringer of the development process, whatever unpredictability it originally had will be gone and most likely it has become predictable. Even worse, it may turn out to be ordinary.

Understand that D-boys and D-girls are part of the system. You'll have to deal with them whether you have an agent or not.

## You're Getting Meetings—Now What?

The biggest problem screenwriters face when they've gotten to the point in their careers where they are actually having meetings is when a meeting is set up to discuss the problems with the script.

It's those "problems with the script" that drive screenwriters out of the business and into the welcoming, nurturing arms of the longshoreman industry.

Surviving these meetings is a matter of understanding what Development Executives want.

The fact is, most don't know what they want. Their purpose is to find good scripts. What's "good"? Should it be commercial? Or artistic? Should it be a nutty comedy, an edgy thriller, a coming-of-age comedy, a teen sex comedy, an old-fashioned romantic comedy, a romantic drama, or something cutting-edge? What does "cutting-edge" mean anyway? Think independent films. Another way of looking at it is like this: If it doesn't play at the cineplex at your local mall, it's edgy.

Maybe a D-girl and D-boy's job is to find "the right vehicle" for a certain actor. If somebody is told to find a funny action/adventure for The Rock, that's what he'll be looking for. Anything that doesn't fall into that genre will be passed over (unless a conscientious person finds a script that she falls in love with and is willing to take a chance and recommend it to the director of development even though the company's looking for that thing for The Rock).

Working with Development Executives is the price a screenwriter must pay to sell a script and then get a movie made. Go into the meetings knowing you will be told to change a script they claim to love or like a lot. You will receive notes that don't make sense, that are contradictory, and that make you doubt your hearing and sanity. Is there anything you can do about it? Not really. If a D-boy or D-girl somewhere claims to like your script and wants you to make changes, take a deep breath, grab your pen, and listen.

If she turns out to be a gem of a D-girl who says everything right, consider yourself lucky. If you get a D-boy who makes no sense, seems to be talking about an entirely different script, and makes you wonder why you ever wanted to be a screenwriter in the first place, you should still consider yourself lucky.

At least someone is showing interest in your script. And if you're really lucky maybe he'll get fired and be replaced by someone who knows her stuff.

## Be Careful Who You Trust

After you've completed your screenplay it's wise to register it with the Writers Guild of America, East or West. You may wish to copyright it as well. Some screenwriters do both; others feel that registering it with the Writers Guild is enough. You can also register treatments and outlines with the Writers Guild.

Now you can feel secure that your screenplay, which has only been seen by your trusted network of friends (maybe three people, probably all screenwriters, and your girlfriend or boyfriend, wife or husband, and a sibling who wants you to succeed).

Registering and copyrighting your screenplay should give you a degree of comfort in that no one will make a blatant attempt to steal your material—probably.

Here's the big but: Once your script is out there it's *really out there*. Alone, like a babe in the woods. If you send it out to lots of people (agents, producers, managers, actors, directors, and underlings of all kinds), your script might get passed around. Or tossed around. Or left someplace.

That exposure can be good. Or bad. If the right person stumbles onto your script at the right time and place, this is cool. But if the bottom-feeder/lowlife/hanger-on gets hold of your screenplay and likes certain parts or decides that the execution sucks, but the concept is great . . . well, this is where it can get scary.

Producers get their money by producing. Just as writing a script that gets bought pays a screenwriter, producers earn their bucks by getting a go-ahead. Once they get a green light they get a salary. This is fine and dandy and how it should be. But when a producer is in desperate need of a payday he may resort to desperate measures to make sure his movie happens. He just might take liberties with your script to make his project look better.

How do you prevent this from happening?

Unless you are 100 percent attached to the project and involved in the setup of the deal and working daily with the producers and talking to them daily, there is the risk that you will be out of the loop when the deal is made.

Just as you know deep down if your girlfriend or wife is cheating on you, you will know if your producer is cheating on you. Suddenly the phone calls stop. You aren't invited to the daily meetings. While he used to call you five times a day, now he doesn't call at all. When you call him he's vague or evasive or not there or tells you that things are moving along.

Assume that if you're being excluded you're (at the moment) off the project. You may be brought back. In fact, you may be brought back on without even knowing you were officially off the project in the first place. If you are off the project, knowingly or otherwise, it may have nothing to do with the merit of your work. It may mean that a new director wants his favorite writer. Or one of the other producers wants his favorite writer. Or they've lost faith in your freshness despite the fact that you've done eleven drafts in which you addressed all their "ideas," good, bad, stupid, or whatever.

It goes back to the fair-haired boy theory. Somebody new and fresh is always more appealing than somebody who's been around, despite the fact that the person has delivered the goods.

Bottom line: Get everything in writing. If you have an agent, she'll take care of that. If you don't, be very careful. Hire an entertainment lawyer to look out for you. Get a letter of agreement or contract of some sort spelling everything out: money, how many drafts you'll do, the exact credit you will receive ("story by" or "written by" or both), rights, and so on. Producers might be able to take your script away from you and rewrite beyond recognition, but don't let them screw you out of a credit. In Hollywood, a credit is everything. Having a movie made is better than not having a movie made, even if the finished product isn't very good. You go up a notch on the screenwriting food chain when you've had a film made.

Everybody connected with the project will take credit for all the good stuff you did anyway. Conversely, if it tanks, they'll all blame you.

There's a good book on protecting yourself called *The Writer Got Screwed (but Didn't Have To): A Guide to the Legal and Business Practices of Writing for the Entertainment Industry,* by Brooke A. Wharton.

Check it out.

I know that I sometimes sound paranoid and suspicious, especially of producers. This is only because I've had some creepy experiences (admittedly, as well as some great experiences) and I have friends who've also been screwed over.

That being said, I heard a great quote recently that pretty much summed up my feelings about the matter. It has to do with dating and marriage and it goes like this:

"Keep your eyes wide open before you decide to marry someone and keep your eyes half-closed after you've gotten married."

How does this apply to the movie business? Before you decide to sign with an agent or manager or do business with a producer, check him out. Try your damnedest to get a feel for him. If it feels right, go for it.

When in doubt contact the Writers Guild. They'll have a list of producers in good standing. However, many fledgling producers, as well as well-established producers, don't work within the Writers Guild guidelines. As a new writer you may find yourself working with these people because they're willing to make your movie. Understand that you won't be paid as much as if you were in the Writers Guild and that you might be taken advantage of (by being asked to do endless rewrites), but if one of these producers is the only one knocking on your door, I say let him in. You can also find out a producer's credits by going to www.imdb.com.

Then, once you're in the "marriage" so to speak, be understanding and try not to become an insecure mess.

You need to know what you're getting into. Date somebody and only see her through rose-colored glasses or deny certain problems and you'll pay the price down the road. Same with that agent, manager, or producer. Everybody looks and sounds good at the beginning. It's the long haul that counts.

## You Scratch My Back and I'll Scratch Yours

There's a saying in legal circles that a judge is a lawyer with a politician for a friend. A lot of people who work in the entertainment industry were clerks at Banana Republic with a friend or relative in the movie business.

When I was starting out I wished I had connections from birth, my father's country club or college. I had to make mine inch by inch. I took one writing class that led me to another, better, writing class that took me somewhere else, and on and on until I got my first agent and started getting my work produced.

Despite having my foot in the door and a pretty good agent, I still had to keep on hustling and schmoozing and making fresh connections. Ironically, I actually became a connection for other people. Know what? I was (and am) happy to do it.

I like helping people hook up with agents or producers (or anyone who can help them). Not because I'm this great guy but because I believe in the whole karma thing. I help somebody. Somebody helps me down the road. It's worked. I've been very fortunate in this area and I encourage everyone I know to be as generous as possible.

Not everyone is. There are a number of people I've encountered who will not help someone else. Not even by allowing a person to use their name as a referral to an agent or producer. I don't understand this behavior. Maybe it's my Midwestern, Catholic upbringing, but it doesn't make sense to me.

Maybe some people are selfish or self-centered or so into themselves that they don't have the internal mechanism to remember when they needed help.

I'm writing about this because somebody helped me recently, simply by recommending me for a writing assignment. The person didn't have to, but she said she did because I had helped her years ago on a project. My help consisted of simply reading her script and giving her some suggestions. She never forgot that. When a situation arose in which a writer had to be recommended, she gave my name.

Be generous.

Be helpful.

It may not pay off all of the time, but sometimes it will.

## Opportunity Knocks Rarely (and Sometimes Softly)

Once you have a couple of scripts under your belt and you're sending them out and maybe getting representation or interest from producers or entering contests and basically leaving no stone unturned in your quest to get a deal, it's easy to be confused and suspicious.

I've had many conversations with new writers who somehow manage to get an agent or manager to show interest in them. Sometimes what happens is that the writer is reticent about signing with someone who "isn't big enough" and misses out on an opportunity. There's something to be said for thinking big. It's probably better to be signed by ICM than a new agent or agency that's been in business for a month. However, it's easy to get lost in the big-agency shuffle. Sometimes it's smarter to go with a new agent who's crazy about your script and passionate about promoting you and getting you meetings.

Remember, every big or hot agent was somebody's assistant at one point in his career. Nobody just steps into a million-dollar deal.

So if you get an offer of representation and that's the only person knocking on your door, you should probably answer it, before the knocking stops.

## What About Your Short Film?

Once you have a short film that has gone through the same process as your screenplay, i.e., you've gotten feedback, shown it to trusted friends and a small, select audience, and spent many hours editing it and reshaping it and you feel that it's a terrific showcase of your directorial skills, you now have to get the right people to look at it.

With a full-length screenplay and your short film in hand, you are not just a screenwriter. You are a writer-director. You want these same agents, managers, and producers to hire you to, ideally, direct your script, or some other script that they're producing.

Getting your short film seen requires the same, if not more, effort as if you were only promoting a screenplay. Again, there's no right, or easy, way to go about this; you just have to do lots of homework.

Enter your short film in contests and festivals. If you're lucky, it'll win something or get noticed. How do you find contests and festivals? Go to the trusty Internet and the various film magazines that are out there. Get as many people to look at your film as possible. You never know who's going to like it enough to recommend it to somebody important.

You also need to find out which agents and managers handle writer-directors as opposed to only screenwriters. How? Again, the Hollywood Creative Directory: http://hcdonline.com. You'll find many agents and managers who handle writer-directors.

The movie business is a strange, weird, dangerous, but ultimately exciting industry. On your way up it can be frustrating, maddening, and heartbreaking, but if you view it as a marathon and you're willing to take the hits that will come (and they will come), you'll find that the journey is also fun, exhilarating, and creatively rewarding.

# Lecture 23

# Stuff to Mull Over (During Writer's Block and Other Dry Periods)

It's all about letting the story take over.
—ROBERT STONE

## When Your Muse Hates Your Guts

You can't wait for your muse to show up. The more deadlines you have, the more you realize that you can't sit around hoping for inspiration. Sometimes you have to make it happen. If you're lucky enough to have a paying job and your deadline is Tuesday, you have to suck it up and get it done. If you don't, you'll get canned and they'll hire somebody who isn't wasting time romanticizing the creative process.

People who work on weekly TV shows have to get a script out each week. They work outrageously long hours. They work until a script is rewritten, even if it's three in the morning. They go home. Come back early. And do it again the next day if necessary. And again the next day. No matter how tired or drained they are, they have to do the work. If the muse isn't there, hope she shows up, but in the meantime, get cracking.

## The Poker Analogy

There's an old saying about poker that goes like this: "It takes five minutes to learn but a lifetime to master." Screenwriting's like that. You can learn the basics of structure and storytelling pretty fast, maybe not in five minutes but in a relatively short time. However, it takes years and years to master it. So if you haven't sold your first, second, fifth, seventh, or tenth script, don't feel sorry for yourself. You're just getting better.

## A Lesson from Comedians

I had an opportunity to go to the Friars Club in New York City when there was a salute to Soupy Sales. If you're too young to know who Soupy Sales is, you might learn something from this story. If you know who he is, then you might get a kick out of it.

The event was to celebrate the publication of a new book by Soupy, a collection of jokes called *Stop Me If You've Heard It!: Soupy Sales' Greatest Jokes.*

But unlike most book signings, there was a ninety-minute show afterward in the Friars Club dining room in which half a dozen comedians each told jokes. Legendary radio personality Joey Reynolds served as master of ceremonies. He would toss out a subject and each comic would tell a joke on it. With the exception of one of the comedians who was perhaps in his forties, the rest were of a certain age. If I didn't know they were comedians—still working comedians, I might add—it would have been easy to assume that they were retired insurance agents, lawyers, or accountants.

In the center of the stage sat Soupy Sales, himself probably in his seventies and not in the best of health. Once the joke telling began, these guys—these grandfatherly type guys who looked so staid and mellow—suddenly became young again. It was like watching hot up-and-coming comics in their twenties.

They had life. Juice. Energy. Passion. The guy I'm assuming was the oldest was the best.

He had to be in his eighties. Maybe older.

But he killed.

I mean, he killed.

The lesson I want to share with you is that it was both humbling and inspiring to see these guys performing. They'd been comics all their lives, some more successful and better known than others, but they were still doing it. And enjoying it.

That's what the screenwriting game has to be like. We all want the high-six-figure deal, but getting WGA minimum isn't bad, either (around fifty thousand). A decent-sized option might keep you going, too. Or maybe a rewrite that brings in some fast cash.

But at the end of the day, you should enjoy the process of writing, the pleasure of creativity, the satisfaction of coming up with a new idea and making it work.

Go Soupy and his buddies!

## Hating Your Work

New screenwriters (or any kind of writer) discover a new experience once they've nearly finished a draft or actually completed one.

---

### Joining the Writers Guild

Don't call them; they'll call you when they're notified by a production company that is a signatory, which means that it abides by the rules of the Writers Guild. Once the guild finds out that you are working with the signatory, the terms of your deal are examined. If you've earned enough to gain entry (usually the equivalent of a half-hour TV episode, approximately eighteen thousand dollars as of this writing) you will be invited to join the guild.

They hate what they wrote.

You will, too! You will absolutely loathe what you've written. And you'll really get down on yourself for having written such junk and question why you even started the project, let alone stuck with it.

Now you've invested too much time to abandon the screenplay, so you show it to a friend or teacher or the script consultant you've hired who has been encouraging you and telling you that you're doing very good work and with the exception of some tweaking here and there and maybe a better-defined end of Act Two event and a strong middle of Act Three surprise you're almost done. Just as actors take acting lessons and singers hire coaches, screenwriters have consultants available to them. Check the Internet and screenwriting magazines for ads and Web sites.

No matter what the level of positive or constructive feedback, you're still in the middle of hating what you wrote.

The solution is to give yourself some time.

Usually we start to hate what we've written right after we *really liked* what we wrote. It's like a hangover. The drinking the night before was fun, but the next morning we're cursing ourselves for having pissed away all that money on booze and all that time on meaningless chatter.

Then the hangover ends and we start the next day with a new and pure sense of being and things don't look so glum. That's how to handle that period when you hate your work. Go with it. Pinpoint what exactly isn't working. Bite the bullet and fix it; then, lo and behold, you'll like it again. Maybe even love it.

It's just how it is.

## Good Versus Great

A new screenwriter I was recently working with asked me this question after I told him his first draft was very good: "What'll it take to make it a great script?"

My answer surprised him. I said that the "greatness" of a script will come down the road. No script, no matter how good when it goes out into the world, will go without being rewritten to suit the feedback of the director, producer, actor, and even writer after he's given his "very good" script some distance.

Scripts that are considered very good when they're bought get rewritten or at least retooled. Same with scripts that are very, very good.

Most scripts get rewritten right before shooting starts. They call this a production rewrite. It's done to fine-tune dialogue, make certain scenes funnier, add shadings and contours to a poorly drawn character, and decide if a scene needs to be embellished or can be cut entirely.

Then there are the revisions that happen on the set when the director or an actor has an idea that nobody else thought of.

Don't wait for perfection. Get your script to a point where it's as good as it can be and then send it to your agent (if you have one) or use it to get an agent. How do you know it's as good as it can be? Ask three people who will read it and be truthful. You want them to tell you what works and what doesn't. Don't ask your girlfriend or boyfriend who likes everything you do. You want a more objective opinion of how good it is.

Worry about the greatness later.

## A Lesson from Pilots

A competent airline pilot needs to know certain things. He has a checklist of stuff that needs to be done before he takes off. He needs to be aware of the weather conditions at the beginning and end of his trip, fueling—and so on.

This checklist mentality is another way of looking at what every screenwriter has to do to stay in the game.

Know your market. Know your genre. Maybe you should rethink

that wacky teen comedy set against the backdrop of the bubonic plague. Are your protagonists too old? Should you really write that love story about the two sweet old people in the nursing home?

Then there's the steps you take before you start the script. Are you a treatment person or an outline person? To me a treatment is fifteen pages and over. To me an outline is three to ten pages. Or do you just start writing (which is something I don't recommend)? Maybe that works for you. But for most people it doesn't. Most of the people I've encountered do some form of prethinking before they begin the writing.

Like a pilot: They have a pretty good idea of how it's gonna end; they know the act breaks, especially the end of Act One. They know most of the complications and obstacles their hero will face. They know a subplot.

Before they take off, they have a workable flight plan.

## A Roll of the Dice

There's no safe way to roll the dice when you play craps.

You can blow on them, have your wife or girlfriend blow on them, shake them a certain way, talk to them before you toss them, or do whatever little ritual you think might make them roll your way.

All you really can do is hope they land on the number you want.

Writing screenplays is like that. Nobody knows which script will go for a million or for scale or be rejected. If you come up with an idea that you love—I mean really love and feel strongly about—there are no guarantees that it'll be any good or that it will sell.

Likewise, if you decide to try to write the crassest, most commercial goofy teen sex comedy there's no guarantee that it won't tickle the right producer's funny bone and sell for half a million and be put on the fast track.

Bottom line: Come up with as many ideas as you can. Sift through them until you find one that really grabs you, then write it. Don't think about whether it will sell. Just enjoy the process of writing it and think-ing it through, do the best you can to make it work, then send it out.

Then start the next one.

## Completion Is Everything

I think getting to the end of your first draft is most important, be-cause then you have a chance to, as my first writing teacher once said, "see what you've written."

Unfortunately, many screenwriters, both new and not so new, never get to that point. They give up at various stages along the way only to start another script with the hope of completing it. Sometimes they do, but more often they don't. So they give up on that one as well.

I'm not saying that you shouldn't give up on a script.

Sometimes it just doesn't work out and needs to be put aside. Sometimes it's one of those ideas that sounded good or felt right at the time but then later on it (and your enthusiasm for it) fizzles out.

Be careful about how often you jump ship. If you start and stop on two ideas, make a promise to yourself to finish the third. Nobody will buy a half-completed screenplay. Nobody will buy your first draft of a completed script, but at least it's done and you can start revising and rewriting and making it better and shaping it into something that an agent might want to handle or a producer might want to option.

The next best thing to writing the words "The End" on a screenplay is writing your name as you endorse a big check from a studio.

## How Much Do You Like to Write?

Let me rephrase that: Do you like writing? Or do you love it? Or do you find the act of sitting down at your computer or desk to be slightly less pleasurable than a colonoscopy?

I like to write. I love getting an idea for a plot twist or coming up with a good line (or a great line). I find it fun and challenging and re-warding.

Here is what Nigerian poet Niyi Osundare says about writing:

*One hasn't become a writer until one has distilled writing into a habit, and that habit has been forced into an obsession. Writing has to be an obsession. It has to be something as organic, physiological, and psychological as speaking or sleeping or eating.*

## Lecture 24

# Avoid People Without a Plan

You do your best work when you're not conscious of yourself.
–PETER MATTHIESSEN

Some people are focused. Some aren't.

What's the old saying about boats? You're either sailing full speed ahead or drifting.

People who don't have a plan get in the way of people who do.

In other words: Choose your friends wisely. Don't spend time around negative people who are jealous of your dream because they don't have anything going on in their lives.

Don't waste time with people who make fun of you for having the audacity to want something huge.

Surround yourself with people like you who love movies and want to be in the business.

Police often refer to something called the Blue Wall of Silence. This basically means that cops tend to associate with other cops because only another cop understands what they go through.

Screenwriters and filmmakers are pretty much like that, too.

## How Many Know-it-alls Do You Know?

In my roles as screenwriting teacher and script consultant, I read more scripts than the average person, which means I give my opinion on whether or not a script works or doesn't on a regular basis.

I've learned to be careful about what I say to an author. I try to be fair and honest. I never (intentionally) come off as the world's-smartest-person-who-knows-everything-there-is-to-know-about-what-it-takes-to-write-a-good-screenplay. I have met people like this.

These are people who think they know best and can read a script and tell you exactly what's wrong with it and how to fix it. As you read what they have to say or listen to their stream of criticism you know two things: They've never actually written a screenplay, and they lack the ability to critique the script *that's been written,* not the script *they* would write if they had the ability.

I recently attended the reading of a play. The play was quite good. It needed work here and there. Maybe it would have benefited from a stronger end of Act One and more shadings and contours for the lead character.

I stuck around for the "discussion" that followed. On the whole I mistrust people who partake in these discussions. Most of them just like to take a dump on somebody else's work and/or hear themselves talk. Of course, there are also those who are too nice, but that's another problem entirely. I'm concentrating on the know-it-alls.

I felt sorry for the playwright.

He had to listen to these elitists tell him how bad his play was and how, if he listened to *them,* it would be greater than *King Lear.*

Needless to say, no postplay discussion group lacks for experts. This poor guy had to listen to contradictory points of view from one pompous ass after another. Only a few people actually gave him useful feedback. (I didn't say a word. I never publicly say anything.)

The few who gave the guy information he could use all said the same thing: "First act ends on a weak note. Could be bigger. You go for a laugh in a few spots where you shouldn't. A couple of characters, especially the lead, could be embellished. The ending came upon us too fast," and they went on to mention a few other specific, fixable points.

The playwright took the criticism like a trooper, but I know he was sick to his stomach when it was over. I've been there, both as a playwright and as a screenwriter. When I gave him my thoughts the next day it was very civilized, specific, and encouraging.

I didn't try to make his play my play. I tried to offer suggestions that would make what he wrote more clear and focused. A couple of things I said might've been off the mark, but I knew that the essence of what I told him was helpful and would be something worth considering when he started the next draft.

Moral of the story: Avoid know-it-alls. They're full of it.

Oftentimes, development people will attempt to do this to screenplays. Your nifty story about the speech-impaired nineteen-year-old female hockey player whose dream is to play on the all-male USA Olympic team can easily be turned into an urban drama about a dyslexic African-American girl who wants to climb Mount Rushmore and dance on Teddy Roosevelt's nose.

Producers and development people are simply doing their jobs, which is to help the screenwriter make a script more appealing to the actors and directors they want to offer key roles to and ultimately to create a film that will have more commercial appeal to an audience. Whether they're right or wrong is out of the screenwriter's hands.

# Lecture 25

# It's Not Who You Know; It's Who You Get to Know

*Write even when you don't want to, don't much like what you are writing, and aren't writing particularly well.*

–AGATHA CHRISTIE

I know a lot of screenwriters at varying stages in their careers. They are friends, acquaintances, former students, current students, colleagues, script-consulting clients, waiters, actors, and parking lot attendants. Some have had movies made, others have gotten deals, and more than a few are on the verge of their big breaks.

Since my book *The Screenwriter Within* was published in 2000, I receive numerous e-mails every week from people who liked the book or from a new screenwriter with a question.

Because I'm in frequent contact with many of these screenwriters I pick up bits and pieces of information, industry gossip, trends, producers and agents to avoid, cool development people, and so on. And just as people share stuff with me, I share with them, even if it's just something like. "I heard that Producer A is looking for an action comedy. Didn't you write one of those four years ago when they weren't buying action comedies?"

You can call this networking, schmoozing, back-scratching, or whatever, but it's important to do and if you're not getting out and meeting other screenwriters and sharing anecdotes, insights, or horror stories you're not being a professional.

All the screenwriters (and TV writers) I know who've sold scripts and gotten deals and even had scripts made, with rare exception, were good at this.

If they had no contacts, they made them by writing letters, making phone calls, sending e-mails. Many times nothing happened. I know people who've sent four-sentence query letters to agents and had them returned unread with a disclaimer stating that the agent is not accepting queries. I mean, the lowest common denominator of getting someone to read your work is a query letter, and if he won't read that, what can you do?

Well, you find a way. There is always a way. It may not work on the first twenty agents or producers you contact, but it might work on the twenty-first.

Every person who has ever gotten a deal didn't go to UCLA Film School or Harvard or NYU. Some people—dare I say, most people—don't know anyone. President Lyndon B. Johnson said the following about making connections in Washington, D.C: "It's not who you know; it's who you get to know."

That's cool.

And smart.

And very sound advice.

You're a screenwriter. Get to know some more people like you. There's safety and comfort in numbers.

If you live in LA, meeting fellow screenwriters is fairly easy, because as the old joke goes, everybody in LA is writing a screenplay or thinking about it.

But if you're anywhere else, especially in a smaller city or suburban town, it's going to be harder to create a screenwriting community. Take an online screenwriting class or join (or start) a screenwriting support group. Find chat rooms seeking out screenwriters of filmmakers. If there are five or six screenwriters in your area you can form a writing group.

Just sitting at the computer and writing makes Jack a very dull screenwriter.

## How Many Producers Do You Know?

As I said earlier, if you have a hard time finding an agent or manager, getting access to producers is a good way to break in.

Again, it means working at it. If not every day, almost every day. What you want to do is find out who is producing movies. You can do this by looking at the movie ads in the Entertainment Section of your newspaper. Write down the names of the people and companies listed as producers.

Suddenly you have a company and maybe a couple of names.

Next you need to find their addresses. Go to the Hollywood Creative Directory or www.scriptsales.com and you'll learn where they are.

Next you have to find an innovative, sexy (I hate using that word) way of contacting them and asking them to read your script. If you can find out a person's e-mail, cool. If all you have is the address, fine. Either way, make your message short.

Having a good Logline is crucial. The Logline is a brief description of what your screenplay is about, ideally one sentence. And your e-mail or letter should be equally spare.

For example:

Dear Producer:
  I've written a comedy about a [fill in your great premise].

I know enough producers to know that if something comes in that falls into the category of a "great" premise or "big" idea, they're more than likely to bite and ask to read the script.

But if your e-mail sentence is something like:

Dear Producer:

   I've written a revisionist historical biopic on the life of Mary Todd Lincoln before she met Abraham.

you won't get anyone's attention.

The point I'm making is that when you're new at this or even if you've been at it awhile, there's the fantasy that you'll get an agent who will send your script to a bunch of places and you'll get a deal. Even if you get an agent, there are no guarantees.

So you need to chase down production companies, because if a producer finds a script, he'll run with it. Or at least he'll like it enough to ask to read your next script. Suddenly you have a relationship. And if you keep in touch with him and he keeps liking your stuff, he may recommend something that's not his cup of tea to another producer.

So now you have two producers to send your stuff to (hopefully until you get an agent or manager).

The object is to get to know as many producers as possible. And that also means getting to know the development people and secretaries who work at the office. Get people to like your work (and you) and you'll be surprised how many contacts you suddenly have. For beginning screenwriters and filmmakers, you should be living in Los Angeles. The prevailing wisdom is that once a screenwriter's career has taken off she can live anywhere and only come to LA for meetings. But when you're getting into the business, it's smart to be out there. The bulk of the production companies are there, as are the studios, agents, and managers. The day will come when you'll have to meet some of these people. If you're in LA you can be available on a moment's notice.

Ideally, it's best to have an agent or manager submitting your work. You're the creative person. You should be spending your time writing. The agent/manager is the business part of your career. They spend their time trying to sell scripts, get their clients assignments, and put together deals. If you can't get an agent or you're dissatisfied with the agent you have, it's up to you make your career happen. Not having an agent or manager has one perk: you don't have to give anyone a commission. Ten percent for agents and 15 percent for managers.

## How Many Actors Do You Know?

Actors can't help you. Unless you've written something that they love and they have the clout to get a movie made, which means they have to be a movie star, and I mean a *huge* movie star, because *small* movie stars don't necessarily have clout, and even *huge* movie stars can't get a project off the ground all that easily.

Actors might be able to help you if they're up-and-coming and they like you and your work (but mainly your work) and they know other actors with a little more clout or an up-and-coming director who's looking for a certain kind of project to do and yours just happens to be the kind of project the guy's looking for, so the actor you know gets the director a script and he loves it and takes it to a studio and suddenly you're in the middle of a deal.

This almost never happens.

Most of the time actors can't help you. Maybe the best you can hope for is that one will recommend you to his agent.

That hardly ever happens, because actors' agents tend not to represent screenwriters.

So concentrate your energy on getting to know agents and producers.

Just so you know, actors tend to be more fun to hang with.

## Last Class

# A Final Exam of Sorts

In everything one must consider the end.
–JEAN DE LA FONTAINE

Those screenwriters and filmmakers fortunate enough to go to a university film school learn more than just the techniques of moviemaking. They also receive a well-rounded liberal arts education.

In the Undergraduate Film and Television Department at NYU we want students to learn more than how to light a shot, block a scene, set up a camera, and write a script. We want students to learn how to think so they can become not only intelligent filmmakers and screenwriters but also introspective, discerning citizens.

Which is why going to a university film school should be the first choice of any young screenwriter and filmmaker.

Whether it's the upper-echelon schools like NYU, Columbia, USC, and UCLA or fine universities like Florida State University, University of Texas at Austin, Duke, and others, if someone is fortunate enough to get into one he'll receive a good education.

There's a lot to be said for studying the humanities, science, world literature, and the arts. How do you put a value on the experience of taking a course devoted to eighteenth-century Irish poets?

*The Portable Film School* has taken you into the world of screenwriting and filmmaking. While you continue to grow as a writer and director, as your last assignment I encourage you to grow in other areas, as well.

Don't just see movies; read screenplays and subscribe to magazines devoted to the film industry. Read novels and nonfiction on a wide range of subjects. Go to the theater. If you can't afford to attend plays, *read* them, especially the classics. Visit museums. Learn to appreciate fine art and music. Read all types of magazines and newspapers.

Know what's going on in the world. Keep current. Travel. See this world. Continue to educate yourself. The more of life you're exposed to, the broader the range of material you can write and make films about.

Not only that, but you will find many new interests that will enrich your life.

I'm not a big C. S. Lewis fan (although I tend to respond to any writer who uses initials instead of an actual name); however, he has a wonderful line that every screenwriter and filmmaker should consider:

*All Joy reminds. It is never a possession, always a desire for something longer ago or further away or still about to be.*

When I heard this I thought about it and I found it life affirming. As with so many things that great thinkers and great writers say, it's open to interpretation.

I choose to apply it this way: I am filled with joy once I get a new idea. I'm filled with more joy as I start to write it. I remember the joy of other ideas that turned into finished screenplays. I recall the hope for the script as I sent it out into the world. And I remember the close calls and near misses and the occasional deal that actually happened.

However, the further into the newest project I get, the less joyous it becomes, and I start to get angry and frustrated.

There is no joy remaining.

Then, somehow, the joy returns as I manage to solve the problems of the script, and as I move forward to completion I get really, *really* joyous about the joy that's about to be.

I love the joy that is "about to be."

My joy is fresh with each new script. My hope is fresh. My aggressiveness is fresh. My determination is fresh.

And as I wait to see how it plays out, I anticipate doing it all over again.

This is what writing is all about. Great hope in the pursuit of your dream.

Good luck with your short film and full-length screenplay.

I leave you with the following thought from John Cheever:

*The point is to finish and go on to the next thing.*

# Resources

## Recommended Reading

*Producing and Directing the Short Film and Video* by Peter W. Rea and David W. Irving.

*Writing the Short Film* by Patricia Cooper and Ken Dancyger.

*The Writer's Journey: Mythic Structure for Writers* by Christopher Vogler.

*Lew Hunter's Screenwriting 434: The Industry's Premier Teacher Reveals the Secrets of the Successful Screenplay* by Lew Hunter.

*How to Sell Your Screenplay: A Realistic Guide to Getting a Television or Film Deal* by Lydia Wilen and Joan Wilen.

*Cool Million: How to Become A Million-Dollar Screenwriter* by Sheldon Woodbury.

*The Film Encyclopedia: The Most Comprehensive Encyclopedia of World Cinema in a Single Volume* by Ephraim Katz.

## Cool Web Sites You Should Know About

The Internet is filled with dozens of Web sites devoted to various aspects of screenwriting, filmmaking, and the film industry. Some are jam-packed with information on screenwriting contests, recent script sales, and helpful tips on breaking into the business.

Others provide names of agents, managers, and producers who'll read screenplays. Some are just plain fun, filled with gossip and opinions from serious film buffs. Once you begin to explore these sites, you'll find links to additional sites and you'll quickly find your favorites. The following are some of mine.

## Screenwriting

- Hollywoodlitsales.com
- Scriptsales.com
- Scriptpimp.com
- Writerstore.com
- Script-o-rama.com
- Scriptologist.com
- Inktip.com
- Wordplayer.com
- Moviebytes.com
- Zzippeddskripptzz.com

## Filmmaking

- Filmmaking.com
- Filmfestivals.com
- Filmmaking.net
- Withoutabox.com
- Insidefilm.com
- Zap2it.com
- Projectgreenlight.com

## Filmmaking Terminology
### Two detailed glossaries of film terms
- www.filmland.com/glossary/Dictionary.html
- http://homepage.newschool.edu/~schlemoj/film_courses/glossary_of_film_terms/index.html

## For Film Buffs

- Imdb.com
- Moviejuice.com
- Aint-it-cool-news.com
- Rottentomatoes.com
- Filmthreat.com
- Filmsite.org

## Excellent Screenwriting and Filmmaking Magazines

- *Creative Screenwriting*
- *Screenwriter*
- *Scr(i)pt*
- *Fade In*
- *Hollywood Scriptwriter*
- *Moviemaker*
- *Screentalk*
- *MovieMaker Magazine*
- *Film Journal*
- *Filmmaker Magazine*

## Film Industry Publications

- *Hollywood Reporter*
- *Variety*
- *Daily Variety*
- *Back Stage*
- *Premiere*
- *The Independent: Film & Video Monthly*
- *Written By* (Writers Guild of America, West)

# Index

# About the Author

D. B. Gilles is the author of the popular screenwriting book *The Screenwriter Within: How to Turn the Movie in Your Head into a Salable Screenplay*. He has been on the faculty of the Undergraduate Film and Television Department at New York University's Tisch School of the Arts since 1991. Gilles began his writing career as a playwright and comedy writer. Four of his plays have been published by Dramatists Play Service, most notably *The Girl Who Loved the Beatles* and *Men's Singles*, which has had numerous productions throughout the world. He has also worked in television creating pilots for CBS and writing scripts for FOX and NBC. Gilles has written several screenplays that have been in various stages of development and production. He is coauthor of the George W. Bush parody *W. The First 100 Days: A White House Journal*. He is also a script consultant and screenwriting coach. Gilles is a member of the Dramatists Guild and the Writers Guild of America. He lives in New York City.

# D. B. Gilles
is available for
## SCRIPT CONSULTATION & COACHING

- Screenplays
- Finished drafts or scripts about to be started
- Treatments (15 pages and up)
- Outlines (1–14 pages)


Check out his Web site
Screenwriterwithin.com
or
contact him directly at
Dbgilles47@aol.com